no garden?
no problem!

Mike Pilcher

no garden?
no problem!

Design and planting ideas for the
smallest of spaces: steps, walls, roof terraces,
balconies, basements and courtyards

David & Charles

ACKNOWLEDGMENTS

I'm indebted to Carole Bickerton for her help with the step-by-step projects you'll find over the following pages, and Justyn Wilsmore for his expertise with a camera. Both exhibited that gardening must-have – great patience.

A DAVID & CHARLES BOOK

First published in the UK in 2002

A catalogue record for this book is available from the British Library.

ISBN 0 7153 1171 9

Book design by Robin Whitecross
Printed in China
by Dai Nippon
for David & Charles
Brunel House
Newton Abbot   Devon

Geometric shapes and spot lighting have been used to great effect in this rooftop fountain.

contents

introduction

You may ask: why write a gardening book for people without gardens? Well, sometimes it's just impossible to ignore those twitching green fingers, and just because you haven't got what most people would call a garden doesn't mean that you're excluded from this most popular of pastimes.

People indulge in gardening for a variety of reasons. Most enjoy the challenge of working with nature to create something individual and beautiful, and there's also the therapeutic effect and the opportunity to enjoy the end results. There's no reason why the lack of a traditional garden should prevent you from experiencing a little bit of this sort of fulfilment. Our homes now tend to be far more individual than they were ten years ago as we all strive to reflect our personal likes and dislikes, and more and more interior designers are using nature as a source of inspiration.

Whether you live in a converted house, an eleventh-floor flat or rented accommodation, *No Garden? No Problem!* will provide you with a wealth of new ideas and practical grow-how. In the past, I've lived in a variety of flats and bedsits but I've always managed to find a way of exercising my passion for garden plants. So, using a hypothetical building as a template, this book takes us on a tour from the basement to the roof to see where in our homes it's possible to grow traditional outdoor plants in a way that's interesting, practical and attractive. The answer is not just in pots, although container gardening is the way to do it, but also in mixing some basic crafts, simple horticultural techniques and an eye for colour and design to produce something that's decorative and fun. If you suspected there was more to it than a hanging basket or windowbox, you'd be right.

Using a few years experience, through meeting many gardeners who have faced just such problems, and by doing a bit of further research, I have written a book that I hope will send you up the garden path. As it says on the cover: 'Discover the garden you thought you didn't have', and enjoy it.

Mike

why garden?

Because it helps to satisfy the body, mind and spirit. Most of us spend our formative years dismissing what our parents do with plants as seriously un-cool. So why do we suddenly realize how enjoyable it is? The answer lies in the fact that, when we try it, we find that the activities of acquiring plants and tending them satisfy a number of our basic human requirements: things we need to do to feel good about ourselves and our environment.

Our early ancestors are often described as 'hunter-gatherers'. These people were cave dwellers who had to hunt to feed and clothe themselves and their families. Next, came the 'farmers', after some bright spark realized that if you stayed in one place, you could cultivate what you needed to survive: this must have seemed a good alternative to being constantly on the move, experiencing skirmishes with other tribes and forever having to build new homes. This was when horticulture was born, and it has been an integral part of our existence ever since.

Nowadays, we can all enjoy public parks and the gardens of stately homes, and our employers often spend thousands furnishing our offices with lush houseplants; there's also plenty of gardening in magazines and on TV, and many environmental projects we can get involved with. But nothing is a true substitute for the pleasure of actually growing something for ourselves at home.

A little gardening will have a positive effect on the well-being of your mind and body. Growing plants is the easiest way of staying in touch with the natural cycles of nature.

body

We all have to strive to cope with our own inadequacies, not helped by the fact that the 'body beautiful' seems to be one of the icons of the twenty-first century, just as it was for the twentieth. While it's sad that so much emphasis is placed on just one aspect of a person's character, it's an unchanging fact of life that first impressions count. Enrolling at the local gym will tone your body but does little, if anything, for the mind, whereas a little regular gardening has a very positive effect on the body, while also reducing mental stress. Any form of physical relaxation is good for you but few are as productive as gardening: a round of golf doesn't put a bowl of delicious strawberries on the table, does it?

get out and get fit

Done sensibly, there's no disputing that gardening is good for our health. There's the cold and wet to contend with in winter, and summer will require an effective sun-block, but on the whole, regular gardening keeps us fitter and healthier and gives us more energy. What's more, looking after our plants becomes part of a routine, so it doesn't seem so much like formal exercise.

If you need any more persuading, doctors and other health advisers advocate half an hour's gardening as a great way of getting fit. They recommend that you should do enough to get warm and slightly out of breath. This may be difficult to achieve if all you're looking after is a couple of houseplants, but if you're cultivating a balcony, roof terrace or porch, then there's bound to be a bit of stair work and lifting involved, all of which will get the heart pumping.

As well as being somewhere that you can get a little exercise and fresh air, your garden is also a place to escape to when you need to relax.

relax and do something

Relaxation doesn't necessarily mean sitting in a chair doing nothing. It's also possible to relax when you're carrying out quite strenuous activities. In fact, some physical exertion in the garden can help to alleviate the stress that you may have built up during the day.

Stress doesn't only affect the mind, it also has a physical effect. It produces an inherited 'fight or flight' response in our body – this means an increased pulse rate, the production of adrenaline and the shutdown of our digestive system. This makes sure we are ready to fight our way out of a situation or that we can run away, should we need to. In times gone by, we would have acted on one of these impulses, but nowadays the physical and chemical responses very rarely have an opportunity to realize themselves (unless we actually do thump the boss or barge our way through the queue at the supermarket checkout). Because of this, these stress hormones build up in the body, resulting in a gradual but marked decline in the effectiveness of our immune systems. This makes us more vulnerable to disease and can make us feel lethargic and generally depressed.

The fact that we spend most of our lives in centrally-heated homes and air-conditioned offices and shops means we stop developing the natural antibodies that are there to help us fight diseases. A regular doses of fresh air will go a long way towards redressing the balance – so getting cold and wet from time to time does have its benefits.

be happy

Another relatively recent phenomenon, Seasonal Affective Disorder (SAD) can also cause lethargy and depression. A lack of natural daylight has been proven to have an adverse effect on our well-being, so in winter we should grab every chance we can to get outside on the balcony, roof or porch for our daily fix of daylight. There's also something very comforting and child-like about looking closely at a swelling flower bud, studying the intricacies of an unfurling leaf and generally watching nature takes its course.

Brilliant colour combinations can go a long way towards enhancing our well-being. Imagine looking out on this orange and blue display on a dismal winter's day.

mind

Since those early years when we inhabited caves and started to grow our own crops, things have changed considerably. As the new millennium unfolds, there's no denying that life has got a whole lot easier. But now we're all in danger of becoming totally self-obsessed. We work too hard and for too long, we exercise less, and stress has become a part of everybody's lives. As a result, our sleep patterns are altered, our moods are changed and our metabolic rates are disrupted. Even the stress of coping with stress has become a common – and potentially life-threatening – problem.

learn something new

One of the best ways to help the mind cope with stress is to divert our attention into a new subject or hobby. We need to create time for a little mental relaxation, time to turn away from our usual routine and think about and do something completely different. Gardening is the answer. Unlike most hobbies and pastimes, it doesn't have to involve other people – family, friends or relatives – so there is less chance for stress to build up because people aren't doing what you want them to do or because they beat you at that game of golf. And if you need proof: in hospitals and day care centres, horticultural therapy is recognized as very successful in the treatment of physical and mental problems. It offers an effective – and drug free – alternative for many seemingly untreatable ailments.

For most people, gardening is a total change from their everyday lives, and it is capable of being both absorbing and entertaining. Some people choose sport, others a language, but more and more are considering gardening as a practical and enjoyable hobby.

Once you start down the gardening path, you will realize what a vast subject it is. Crossing over into the realms of physics, history, geography, art, languages and many other scholarly subjects, it's a hobby that broadens the mind – but only to the degree you want it to. Everyone can garden. It's not the preserve of experts, those with green fingers, or our parents or grandparents. We can do a lot with just a little knowledge. Even the novice gardener can have instant success. Decide to learn a new language, and it's months before you can hold anything like an intelligent conversation. Sow a packet of seed, and you have plants to play with in just a couple of weeks.

Stick with it and you'll start to learn new skills: simple propagation techniques that can produce free plants and pruning at the right time to produce more flowers. Most important, you'll find that growing and caring for something creates a tremendous sense of achievement.

zen

Of all the 'self-help' remedies for coping with stress, meditation is one of the easiest and most successful, if only because it involves sitting, breathing properly and clearing our minds. It is a chance to rest, relax and recharge. When we meditate, we need something to focus on: a suitable subject is found in the minimalist rock and gravel gardens associated with Buddhist monks. Often created in a small, enclosed space and designed to be viewed from an adjacent room, these Zen gardens are a celebration of nature, to be contemplated at length. Whereas the western approach to gardening has been to tame nature's exuberance into contrived borders and formal lawns, putting

This garden at the Chelsea Flower Show captures the essence of a Japanese garden, being both thought-provoking and serene.

plants and materials into a totally alien environment, the Zen ideal is much more natural, achieving a balance of materials (stone, water and plants), light and shade, structure and form. Every rock has a meaning and works together with the adjacent elements. Again, it is providing something to think about, to rest awhile and admire.

While the purist's Zen garden may contain a lot of symbolism and precise theory that is difficult to understand, the basic principle is a good one to follow: plants and natural elements can be used to aid contemplation, diffusing the stresses of everyday life by focusing our minds on something very positive and real. This is one benefit we can introduce to our homes, even if we are denied access to a traditional garden space. Miniature Zen gravel gardens, or Karesansui, are primarily created as works of art but there's no reason why we cannot recreate something similar in our homes, perhaps using a tray of gravel, a beautiful piece of stone and a plant or two.

feng shui

Next, there is our fascination with everything to do with the ancient art of Feng Shui. Basically it's all about channelling the earth's natural energies in a positive way to enhance health, wealth and well-being. Interior designers in the west have started to embrace these principles, and even hotels and retail outlets now bring in Feng Shui experts to create welcoming and productive environments. Although their intentions may be purely commercial, there's no disputing that the basic principles they are working with are a mixture of common sense and sound reasoning, and they seem to work. The aim is to facilitate a flow of positive energy (or chi) around the home, and achieve a balance that suits the location and the needs of the individual. It's not a strict process and there are no hard and fast rules like there are with Zen gardens.

---

feng shui tips

containers should be curved or rounded, rather than square with sharp or angular corners.

shiny containers will help reflect positive energy back into the room.

avoid plants with pointed leaves or thorns as they give off negative chi.

avoid plants with drooping leaves or branches as they send positive chi down into the ground.

cut off any dead and dying flowers and shoots as soon as you see them. Dead plants encourage negative chi, as do plants that are covered in dust and need cleaning – dried-flower enthusiasts be warned.

use plants to energize dead corners of a room where positive energy may stagnate.

one large plant has a more positive effect than an untidy group of different plants in a motley collection of pots.

Feng Shui is increasingly being applied to gardens and the use of foliage, and Feng Shui experts have much to say about living plants in and around the home. While there are many people who are more qualified than myself to write on the subject, and plenty of good books available, the tips below may be helpful.

spirit

Our spirit is what's gives us character, but in a world where we have to conform to personal and professional conventions, our individuality is one of the first things to suffer. Whether we're self-employed, a housewife or a player in a giant conglomerate, it's very easy to feel we're a very small cog in a large, unyielding machine.

In our quest to nurture the spirit, our homes and gardens are becoming much more important to us. They can be an enclave from the strains of the outside world, and a place where we are free to express and practise our personal tastes and lifestyles.

For the would-be gardener, the freedom of expression can manifest itself in a variety of ways – a collection of houseplants that are all members of the same family, a range of exotic plants or a selection of those that have architectural lines and are used more as furniture than floriculture. The aesthetic value of plants shouldn't be underestimated – a single fine specimen can have as much presence as a fine antique or latest designer furniture.

self expression

How the plants are displayed – modest, bizarre, outrageous, subtle – speaks volumes about the person who arranged them. In this, the containers chosen and the planting combinations are as important as the plants themselves. Whatever form the plant displays take, their care fulfils our need to nurture something and see it mature. It's a form of personal fulfilment by proxy if you like, and there's nothing wrong with that. It's probably a much healthier option and less doomed to disappointment than using your kids for the same ends.

ionic balance

At a fundamental level, plants can also have a dramatic effect on our moods. A room containing plants and flowers seems to lift the spirits. The reason for this can be traced back to the effect the plants have on the atmosphere. Not only do they add humidity, but they also

release negative ions, which, contrary to their name, have a very positive effect on how we feel.

Positive ions – associated with cigarette smoke, pollution and synthetic materials – are bad. If they predominate in a room, the occupant will start to feel lethargic, get headaches and be more prone to depression. Negative ions attach themselves to positive ions, dragging them to the ground. Room ionisers, which are sold to 'refresh the air', produce negative ions. Plants do the same, bringing negative ions from the earth and releasing them into the atmosphere. Water has a similar effect, so even a small pool or wall fountain can lift the spirits.

Scientists believe that we feel exhilarated in wide, open spaces and by large volumes of water because this is where the negative ion concentration is naturally high. Whether you agree with this theory or not, there's no denying that just the presence of a plant in a room can make you feel good. And if those plants are a substitute for a garden, then they'll do a lot to satisfy a need and fulfil an ambition, until that craving can be fully realized when we decide, or are able, to move on.

nature's rhythm

Human beings are becoming increasingly removed from the cycles of nature, but it's still a basic human need to know where we are in relation to the seasons. Despite this, we are spending more time indoors, either working or pursuing leisure activities, we travel to work by car, bus or train, and we very rarely walk anywhere where we can observe the changing seasons. This isolation from nature is even more likely if we're confined to a flat in an inner city location.

Even if they are inside our homes, plants are governed by the seasons – flowering plants will cease to bloom when there's insufficient light, and plants stop growing altogether when the temperatures drop too low – and the fact that they change as the year progresses helps to ground us in nature's order. Bedding plants are a particularly good way to keep in touch with the changing seasons, as they have a clearly defined period of growth, flowering and fading. Similarly, there's little to match the excitement of seeing a seed germinate or a cutting produce a healthy flush of roots.

Nature's an incredible thing, and even more compulsive if we can give it a helping hand. By doing so, not only are we improving our own surroundings, we are also enhancing the neighbourhood and doing our bit for the global environment. In New York there are over 750 community gardens where people can go and work with plants and soil even if they haven't a garden themselves. In one of the loudest, brashest and busiest cities in the world, it's interesting to see that people still have the need to garden, and have contrived space to do it in. Attracting over 5000 tourists each year, these community gardens are one form of inner city development that everyone applauds. Utilizing derelict land that may be earmarked for development in the long term, the gardeners are enhancing the environment to the common good.

sensory perceptions

Few hobbies manage to stimulate all the senses so easily as gardening does. On the face of it, it seems to be a visual thing, with the sense of smell catered for from time to time. Think about it a little deeper: it actually affects all five senses – sight, hearing, taste, smell, touch.

sight

Sight is our most immediate sense, which is why we pay particular attention to decorating our surroundings. And plants used as an integral part of the interior design can be changed more easily than wall colours and floor surfaces. Swap a leafy ficus for an architectural cactus and you've changed the style of a room in seconds. A change in the plants involved in your interior design can create a dramatic new look for very little effort and outlay.

Since the beginning of the twentieth century, educationist and social philosopher Rudolf Steiner's thoughts on the effects of colour have been widely accepted and are used in many ways today, often in

colour codes

red An energizing colour associated with love and fertility.

orange An active colour giving energy and enjoyment.

yellow Promotes intellectual stimulation and produces a feeling of well-being.

green A colour of regeneration and hope; a calming influence.

blue Encourages relaxation, a feeling of space, peace and order.

violet Promotes a feeling of self-worth, inspiration and insight.

conjunction with traditional medicine. Colour therapy is used to treat
a number of common complaints, particularly those associated with
stress. This is why major companies, with a vested interest in the
well-being (and performance) of their employees, pay particular
attention to the colours they choose to decorate office and communal
areas. Retail outlets do the same, but use colours that are believed to
help sell. Colours influence how we feel, how we think, even our
personal relationships. Incredibly, the average person can distinguish
between over 10 million different colours and hues, although it never
seems like that when we're buying a tin of touch-up paint.

We all have favourite colours, but how often do we sit down and
really think about how that colour makes us feel? Probably never.
Preferences are built up over the years as colours become linked
with events and memories; they are also dictated by changing
fashions. Flowers, foliage, even pots and gardening accessories can be
used to add colours to the home that will influence our moods.

Movement should also be planned for – a breezeless garden is a
rarity. Swaying branches can have a mesmeric effect and this is one
aspect of the garden that is often at its best when the weather's at
its worst. Other elements also add movement to relax and soothe: a
babbling stream, perhaps, or the gently nodding heads of spring
bulbs. Native plants will attract birds and insects to the garden,
flitting about before our eyes as they go about their daily business.

hearing

The second sense we have to play with is that of hearing. Apart
from the obvious sounds of nature, like splashing rain and dawn
birdsong, noises can be encouraged into the garden to provide their
own form of 'audio therapy'.

Plants such as bamboo and ornamental grasses with stems and leaves
that rattle in the wind are an obvious choice. If there's one fault we're
all guilty of it's not listening. Good listeners are hard to find, but will
benefit from everything they hear. Spend a moment or two listening
now and I'll bet you'll hear sounds you never realized were there.
Tuning in to nature will make us all much better human beings.

taste

So much of life's little pleasures rely on our sense of taste. For the
gardener this usually translates to the healthy enjoyment of fresh

vegetables, fruit and herbs. However, look a little further and there
are even more remarkable and new tastes to be experienced. Take
nectar as an example – the food of the gods. Tap the stem of some
flowers and this sticky sweet liquid will spill out onto our hands.
Taste it and you will understand what the butterflies and bees have
been keeping to themselves.

Of course it's not a good idea to go round eating everything in the
garden. Many plants are unpalatable and some are extremely poisonous.
But the adventurous gardener who is willing to do a little research, will
find many new tastes to enjoy in his or her beds and borders.

smell

Smell is widely thought to be the most powerful sense, and also one of
the most sophisticated. Everybody has smelt something that has
immediately evoked an image from the past – pleasant or otherwise. In
the confines of a small space, smells will be concentrated and linger in
the air longer: the urban gardener with a single potted lily will

Star jasmine (*Trachelospermum jasminoides*) has intensely fragrant flowers. It appreciates a sheltered site where its fragrance will be even more potent.

experience as much pleasure as the landed gentry with complete borders of the things. Planning for scent is important and can be achieved for every day of the year. In fact some of the sweetest smelling plants are those that flower in the depths of winter, when they have to work harder to attract pollinating insects.

touch

Finally, there is touch – something all gardeners do without thinking. Many non-gardeners also do it. Whether we touch because looking alone doesn't produce full appreciation of what we see, or whether it's because the plant's texture says 'stroke me' or 'keep off', this sense is a powerful tool for the garden designer and one that should be exploited.

Of course, touchability doesn't just apply to plants. Hard landscape materials are also there to be felt and enjoyed. The cool, silky smooth surface of a piece of dressed stone or the jagged profile of an aggregate mulch can be as fascinating to the fingers as the most fragile flower or downy leaf. Children learn a lot through touch; it's a sense that educates us even when we don't realize we're using it.

finally

Adding plants to our homes is a form of self-expression; combining an interest in plants with other hobbies makes this self-expression even more fulfilling. For example, if you like to travel, you will enjoy the fact that a wide range of plants from foreign climes will grow quite happily in and around your home. What could be better than growing an orchid that you first saw on holiday in South America or a cactus you glimpsed in its native habitat on the Canary Islands? Inspiration for displaying plants can come from an interest in painting – you can customize the pots they grow in. Or, if you like order, miniature bonsai trees will satisfy those controlling green fingers. However, you can choose your plants simply because their flowers or foliage will enhance the the room they're in. Whatever the reason you grow plants, they will fulfil a human need and provide a great deal of pleasure and fun in the process.

metallic

Interior designers have a continuing passion for metallic colours and it's a look that can easily be incorporated into our planting schemes. There is a wealth of plants that have that essential silver or bronze look.

silver stunners...

Artemisia 'Powis Castle' (wormwood) A shrubby perennial with feathery leaves and yellow flowers in late summer.

Astelia chathamica A broad-leaved evergreen perennial with white-scaly reverses to the leaves. It produces greenish-purple flowers in summer.

Eryngium giganteum (Miss Willmott's ghost) Spiky leaves and silvery thistle-like flowerheads. This is one for a larger pot because of its deep main root.

Eryngium variifolium This is a spiky-leafed evergreen perennial with silvery-white, thistle-like flowers in late summer.

Festuca glauca (grey fescue) An evergreen grass with silvery-blue leaves.

Helichrysum italicum var. *serotinum* (curry plant) An evergreen and very 'fragrant'. This is a neat grower with yellow flowers in summer and autumn.

Helichrysum petiolare This silver-leaved evergreen needs protection from the cold and damp. It is ideal for summer bedding in pots and baskets.

Santolina chamaecyparissus (cotton lavender) A compact plant with woolly foliage. Yellow flowers appear on wiry stems in late summer.

Sedum spathulifolium 'Cape Blanco' (stonecrop) This is a superb mat-forming, fleshy-leaved perennial with minute rosettes of white-powdered leaves. Yellow flowers appear in summer.

Senecio cineraria A shrubby annual that may survive the winter outside. There are many forms, including 'Alice', with deeply cut leaves, and 'Silver Dust', with almost white, filigree leaves.

bronze beauties...

Acer palmatum 'Dissectum Atropurpureum' A cut-leaved maple with a delicate and spreading habit.

Bergenia 'Ballawley' (elephants' ears) This low-growing perennial has evergreen leaves that turn rich bronze in winter.

Cercis canadensis 'Forest Pansy' (redbud) A moderate-sized tree with large, bronze, heart-shaped leaves.

Cotinus coggygria 'Royal Purple' (smoke bush) A large, woody shrub with deep purple-bronze foliage and fluffy flowers in summer.

Hebe 'Amy' A rounded, evergreen shrub with bronze new leaves and purple flowers in summer.

Leucothoe fontanesiana 'Scarletta' (switch ivy) This evergreen shrub has purple young shoots that turn bronze in winter.

Phormium tenax 'Bronze Baby' (New Zealand flax) A dwarf variety which has superb leaves that tip over at the ends.

Pittosporum tenuifolium 'Tom Thumb' An evergreen shrub with glossy, wavy-edged leaves. This is an excellent foliage plant, ideal for cutting.

Ricinus communis 'Impala' (castor oil plant) A shrubby annual with large, deeply lobed, dark bronze leaves.

Rodgersia podophylla A superb herbaceous perennial that prefers a moist spot. The large leaves are bronze as they emerge in spring.

Rodgersia podophylla has attractive architectural leaves and sprays of creamy flowers.

door

Set the mood with stylish pots, hanging baskets or a range of easy-care plants. Like it or not, there's no denying that humans are full of preconceptions and if there is little else to go on, visitors will form their first impression of us from the entrance to our home. Be it modern minimalist or traditional suburban, the style, colour and general condition of that all-important front door will quickly give someone an idea of what lies beyond, the type of person you are, and how much pride you take in your surroundings and the environment.

For those of us living in terraced houses, converted flats or smaller properties, the front step may be the only bit of outdoor space we can call our own. It might be small, very public and cursed with the most inhospitable growing conditions imaginable, but it is still a space that can be used as a garden.

Many of us share an entrance, perhaps to an older property that has been converted into flats. Often depressingly unloved, these places are frequently a general dumping ground for bags of rubbish and abandoned bikes. This makes it even more important to brighten the area up with something vaguely horticultural. In such circumstances, however, I'd advocate consulting your neighbours first before doing anything. You might find that there is a wall of opposition, which will be better dealt with face to face now, rather than via a lawyer's letter later. Most reasonable people, even if they have no interest in what you are doing or in

getting involved themselves, will realize that it's going to make their own environment a little more attractive, and may well add value to their home. Indeed, when it comes to selling, it is an acknowledged fact that an attractively planted front step or hanging basket will give your home the edge over identical properties in the same neighbourhood. It is also surprising how often initially uninterested neighbours, who scoffed at your plans, will come to appreciate the improvements you have made. They might even offer to lend a hand with maintenance. Pride in our environment is something that needs fostering, and if we can start the ball rolling, then so much the better.

The wider the steps, the greater the range of possibilities.

growing environment

If gardening is about being in tune with nature, then it's good to change the look as the seasons progress, but one overriding factor should be taken into consideration and that's the conditions the plants will have to endure. Choose them accordingly and they'll not just survive, they'll flourish, even with the minimum of care and attention.

Thresholds seem to fall into two basic growing environments: those that are baked by the sun, and those that are in almost permanent shade. Each creates a climate that could be a problem but which can be turned into an advantage with a little forethought and planning. Plants for a sunny doorstep should be those that can cope naturally with hot, dry climates and extreme temperature fluctuations. Look for those whose ancestral roots trace back to warmer, harsher climates. These are the ones that will grow easily, require less attention and produce the best flower and foliage display. And for those doorsteps in almost total shade? Here is an opportunity to grow plants from cooler climates, those that prefer dappled or permanent shade and probably originate from more temperate climates, woodlands and forest fringes. These are the plants that will favour a more limited temperature range, moister atmosphere and gentle, diffused light.

Wind can be a problem, in both shady and exposed situations, and should be taken into consideration. In a sunny spot, it can increase the water evaporation rate and very quickly desiccate leaves and new shoots. In shade, the effect is similar but less critical. Shade cast by buildings usually means that winds will be more gusty and so physical damage is more likely.

making a start

I doubt that anyone with a front step will be blessed with superb plantable soil. Most of us have an area the size of a couple of paving slabs to play with – indeed it may be just two paving slabs – and those who actually do have a slip of soil may do better to cover it with gravel: in such locations I have yet to find soil that doesn't

contain a quantity of builder's rubble and hasn't been walked on and compacted over the years into something resembling concrete.

There are two possible plans of attack: dig over the soil as deeply as possible, removing the bricks, stones and roof slates, and incorporating as much well-rotted compost as possible, or cover the soil with a decorative mulch and plan the planting on top. I'd always go for the latter, as container plantings can be more imaginative and lend themselves particularly well to doorways. True, they will require a little more looking after, but the frustrated gardener will relish the chance to water, feed, prune and groom as often as possible.

Undoubtedly, the main reason why containers have become universally popular is because it's probably the only area of gardening where the gardener is in total control. We can chop and change the plantings as easily as personal preferences dictate. There are plenty of small trees and shrubs that can be used as feature plants, and a wealth of compact and more floriferous annuals, perennials and bulbs that are ideal for adding seasonal colour. Containers offer instant gratification. They're quick and easy to plant and we don't have to wait months, or even years, for them to mature.

choose your style

The architectural style of the entrance is always a good place to start when planning what to do. Entrances can have an austere formality, best complemented with equally formal plantings, architectural plants and clipped topiary, or they may be more quaint, lending themselves

Left: Rice-paper plant (*Tetrapanax papyrifer*) makes a bold statement by this back door.

Above right: Don't be afraid of experimenting with bright colour combinations.

TIP Turn containers by doors or walls occasionally so they grow evenly and do not become lopsided

to relaxed or romantic plantings. Colour schemes are often best chosen to match the paintwork or wall colours, giving the whole area cohesiveness. This is the simplest of design tricks but one that always works, and works well.

With many and varied styles of containers available, it's always possible to find something that complements or contrasts with the existing fixtures and fittings. But don't feel confined to using traditional pots for a traditional setting: sometimes a stark contrast in styles is most effective. If you have a contemporary home in a traditional building, make a point of creating something modern on your front step to reflect your personal tastes and individual style of living. Interior design is now about combining the 'old' with the 'new' so why not do the same with your plants?

choosing containers

Look for pots that are interesting shapes, made from attractive materials or have an exciting colour or texture. It's worth spending a little more on good quality containers as they'll look better and last longer. Plainer pots can always be jazzed up with some home decoration. If you have room for a wall bracket, then hanging pots and baskets are an additional option – and a chance to show off your horticultural expertise, now that informal competition for the best hanging baskets seems to have become a healthy obsession in many streets and avenues.

think big

Larger pots are always better than small ones. Not only are they easier to plant and maintain, they're also harder to lift, so less likely to get stolen. In any case, it is always best to anchor specimen plants to their pots or the wall behind, using wires. This will keep them more stable and may deter an opportunist thief. Expensive containers and their contents have become the target of thieves and there is little you can do to eliminate the problem completely. Making sure your front step is well lit at all times will help. Mark your pots with your postcode, name or address, somewhere discrete but permanent so they can be identified should they be stolen and subsequently recovered. There are also various security anchoring devices on the market that can be used to attach a pot to the ground or building nearby.

Left: Larger and fewer pots create greater impact by a front door.

Above right: Roses and clematis produce a cottage-garden atmosphere.

it's a year-round thing

Many gardeners make great efforts to concoct fabulous summer containers, brimful of bedding and bursting with colour. However, come the first frosts and long, dark days of winter, they seem to be happy to look out on a pot full of dead stems and decaying foliage. If only more people took the opportunity to grow some of the superb winter and spring flowers and foliage that are now available in garden centres and DIY stores. There's no reason why a winter container shouldn't be just as colourful as its summer incarnation. Coloured stems, leaves and berries will all brighten up the darkest, dismal days.

make a feature of it

I have to admit that I'm a bit of a lazy gardener and if there's a simple or quick way of doing something, then that's the one for me. It's also my belief that most people are the same – so don't be coy. This is the reason why, in each of my containers, I try to have a few long-term plants that can grow and mature as the season's progress. These feature plants are generally evergreen, usually an interesting shape and may well contribute flowers, fruits, autumn colour or winter interest to the rest of the scheme. They live permanently in large pots and the soil around their base is planted with more transient subjects that change as quickly as the seasons. Spring bulbs, summer bedding, autumn berries and winter foliage ensure that the pots are looking their best at any time of year – and for whoever comes to the door.

light fantastic

A stylish modern planter that also acts as a house number and security night light.

A few years ago you'd have been hard pressed to find a light in many gardens. Now, thanks to the advent of competitively-priced and safe, low-voltage systems, it's quick and easy to install our own. Used to highlight plants, illuminate paths and steps or deter unwelcome visitors, garden lights open up a completely new facet of the gardener's world.

For maximum impact, this planter uses some of the latest materials, combined in a contemporary style that looks equally at home on a modern door step or outside a country cottage. I used a terracotta pot for its clean, straight lines, but a plastic pot would be equally good, perhaps one you already have that could be given a new lease of life? I also experimented with crushed compact discs – just one of a wide range of materials that are being recycled for use as decorative garden aggregates. It's a way of creating impact that will catch the natural sunlight or can be illuminated for a really spectacular night-time welcome.

you will need:

pot
PVA glue
crushed CD aggregate
safety glass – edged for
  easier handling
outdoor spray paint
spray etch
low-voltage spotlight
masking tape
paint brush
newspaper

TIP Working on a sheet of newspaper will allow you to gather up the spare aggregate for reapplying.

1 Spray the container with the oudoor spray paint to create an interesting base. This will show through the aggregate so select a colour that contrasts or tones with it.

2 Cover the pot with a generous coat of PVA glue.

3 Start to apply the crushed CD aggregate. Work quickly, dabbing on handfuls at a time.

4 Once you have worked around the whole pot, throw more aggregate at the surface to fill any holes and leave some sticking out at acute angles to catch the light.

5 Thoroughly clean the sheet of glass before marking out your house name or number with masking tape. You may find it easier to draw out your design on a sheet of paper and place this under the glass to use as a guide.

6 Spray on the glass etch sparingly and evenly. It's better to build up several coats rather than apply one thick one that may run.

7 Leave the etch to dry thoroughly before carefully peeling off the masking tape.

As day turns to dusk, this house number shows up clearly.

light fantastic

The planting was designed around a colour theme of orange, yellow, lime-green and purple. Plants were chosen as much for their foliage interest as their flower colour. Flowers tend to come and go, but foliage has a longer period of interest – particularly if it is evergreen.

you will need:

crocks
good quality multi-
    purpose compost
1 *Crocosmia* 'Canary
    Bird'
1 *Cupressus
    macrocarpa*
    'Goldcrest'
1 *Eucomis bicolor*
    (pineapple flower)
2 Heuchera
1 *Hosta gracillima*
    'Variegata'
2 *Viola* x *wittrockiana*
    Universal Series
    (orange pansies)

TIP As you have total control over the watering and feeding regime, pack in as many plants as possible. This way you can create more interest and greater impact. Water absorbing gel could be added to the compost in spring and summer. Gels act like a sponge, absorbing water and gradually releasing it back into the surrounding compost and roots as needed. The roots of plants sitting in too much water are prone to rotting and those that don't get enough will shrivel and die. Gels make it easier to strike the right balance.

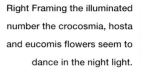
Right Framing the illuminated number the crocosmia, hosta and eucomis flowers seem to dance in the night light.

1 Put a drainage layer of crocks in the bottom of the pot and position the glass panel. Secure it with a couple of bricks at the base so it stands upright. Top up with good quality multi-purpose compost, making sure it's moist when you start. Dry compost can be difficult to re-wet and it will rob your plants of any moisture they contain.

2 Place your main feature plant first – in this case a beautiful lime-green *Cupressus macrocarpa*. Conifers are ideal for containers as they have a fine, fibrous root system and provide a structural, evergreen focal point.

3 Fill in around the conifer, positioning the largest plants first and then adding annuals, foliage and ground-cover subjects.

4 Insert the low-voltage spotlight so it is angled up towards the back of the etched glass panel.

5 Fill in any gaps with more compost, firm well, then top off with a mulch of aggregate. This will help keep the plants clean and shows them off to full advantage.

care & attention

- Containers on front steps, baskets hanging close to walls or under a overhanging porch will need regular watering throughout the year – more in summer and less in winter when growth slows or stops completely.

- Deadhead flowering plants regularly to prevent energy being wasted in seed production.

- Don't be afraid to trim plants during the growing season. Lax growers such as trailing ivies and nepeta will particularly benefit, producing lush new growth rather than long straggly strands.

- Remember to feed container plants. Dense planting and rapid growth mean that nutrients in the compost will be used up rapidly. Liquid feed every two weeks during the growing season. Start with high-nitrogen feeds to encourage robust leaf growth and then switch to a high-potash feed in late spring or early summer to encourage flower production.

seasonal combinations

Change doorstep plantings to reflect the changing colours of the seasons.

spring
Fresh green and pale yellow

Top: Narcissi are the epitome of spring. Here 'Têtê-a-têtê' is complemented by the hyacinth 'Blue Delft'.

summer
Blue, crimson and deep purple

Blues and purples, including clematis, scabious, petunia and violas, are used to create a cool display.

autumn
Orange, burgundy and brown

Dahlias and chrysanthemums combined with cordyline, begonias and a fuchsia, capture the colours of autumn.

winter
White and pink

Less is definitely more in this eyecatching container planted with *Skimmia reevesiana*.

door plant gallery

welcoming scent

Situated by a door or open window, scented plants can really bring the garden into the home. In the evening, when the air is warm and still, their scents will be stronger – just when there's time to enjoy them.

ten fragrant plants...

Buddleja davidii Kept well pruned each year immediately after flowering, this large shrub is hard to beat for its honey perfume. Butterflies love it too.

Convallaria majalis (lily of the valley) This spring favourite has lush green leaves and sweetly scented, white, bell-shaped flowers. Look out for 'Albostriata' with its attractively striped leaves.

Cosmos atrosanguineus An interesting perennial both for its sweet scent of chocolate and its deep maroon flowers. Needs winter protection.

Lavandula angustifolia (English lavender) The mainstay of many fragrant gardens, lavender is available in some excellent named varieties with interesting flower colours. All do well in pots, preferring the free-draining conditions. Look out for the more compact varieties 'Hidcote' and 'Loddon Pink'. French lavender (*L. stoechas*) is also compact enough for a pot and interesting for the bracts on top of each flowerhead.

Lilium candidum (Madonna lily) This magnificent lily has stems carrying 10–15 white trumpet flowers. The plants are unique among lilies in that they produce a cluster of basal leaves in winter so are easy to spot and don't often get accidentally planted over or dug up. For semi-shade, try the equally fragrant *L. longiflorum* (Easter lily), which is also well suited to pot culture.

Lonicera periclymenum (common honeysuckle) Honeysuckle is ideal for training up a wall or trailing over a balcony. 'Belgica' (early Dutch honeysuckle) has white flowers that turn yellow, while those of 'Serotina' are cream with dark purple streaks. Plants can be pruned to keep them within bounds and are happiest in shade.

Magnolia grandiflora A magnificent, but large, evergreen shrub that will relish a warm spot against a wall. Flowers the size of dinner plates are white and heavily scented. The leaves are spectacular, too.

Nicotiana sylvestris (tobacco plant) The largest of the ornamental tobacco plants, with a large cluster of basal leaves and tall stems carrying white, tubular flowers. Prefers partial shade as the flowers close in full sun.

Rosa 'L'Aimant' A vigorous, cluster-flowered bush rose, with salmon-pink, ruffled petals. This is one of the sweetest smelling of all roses, although there is a multitude to choose from.

Sarcococca humilis (sweet box) This easy-to-grow small, glossy evergreen shrub has small but very fragrant, white flowers in winter. The flowers are excellent for cutting to bring indoors.

Above: Welcome guests with the smell of chocolate by planting *Cosmos atrosanguineus* close to the front door.

TIP Cut a few flowers to bring inside. In a cool room, they'll last well and perfume the air.

Above: *Lavandula stoechas* has everything – colour, fragrance, intriguing flowers and pretty foliage – and is great in a pot.

for summer and autumn interest try...

Agapanthus

Allium

Colchicum

Crinum

Crocosmia masonorum

Cyclamen

Galtonia candicans

Gladiolus nanus

Ixia

Lilium

Nerine bowdenii

Sparaxis tricolor

Sternbergia lutea

Tigridia

beautiful bulbs

Pre-packaged by nature and just bursting to come into growth, flowering bulbs are the novice gardener's best friends. They're inexpensive and a simple way of giving an existing planting a bit of a seasonal boost.

eight spring bulbs...

***Anemone blanda* (wood anemone)**
The beautiful woodland anemone is perfect for surrounding specimen shrubs, where it will flower early, producing a carpet of white, pink and mauve.

***Colchicum* (autumn crocus, naked ladies)** These bulbs got their common name of naked ladies because the flowers come up before the leaves. Look out for the perfect white *C. speciosum* 'Album' or the double pink *C.* 'Waterlily'.

Eranthis hyemalis* (aconite)*** The low-growing aconite has butter-yellow flowers and ruff of bright green bracts.

***Fritillaria imperialis* (crown imperial)**
A large bulb with magnificent heads of orange, red or yellow, hanging bells. 'Aureomarginata' has green leaves with yellow edges.

***Galanthus nivalis* (snowdrop)** The simple snowdrop needs no introduction. It is best planted when in leaf as the bulbs can quickly dry out.

Hycinthus (hyacinth) For a heady scent, these bulbs are hard to beat, and equally at home in outdoor pots or in a cool room indoors. Tall flowers may collapse so need precautionary staking.

Narcissus (daffodil) Only the humble daffodil, but still well worth

For spring, and some instant sunshine, plant aconites (*Eranthis hyemalis* 'Guinea Gold'), which thrive in dappled shade.

growing. Bulbs are cheap to buy and flower freely – sometimes with several flowers per stem, and several stems per bulb. Check out the large border types and miniatures like *N. cyclamineus* and *N. bulbocodium*.

Tulipa (tulip) The most flamboyant of the spring bulbs in a wide range of heights, colours and forms. Plant in late autumn for the following spring; subsequent shows are less spectacular so discard the bulbs after flowering.

> **TIP** Don't cut off any bulb foliage until it starts to show signs of dying back naturally. The goodness from these leaves is needed to build up the bulb for next year. Leave at least six weeks before cutting it off.

clambering climbers

Walls adjacent to main doorways or posts supporting porches are the perfect place to grow a couple of choice climbers.

how about...

***Akebia quinata* (chocolate vine)**
Semi-evergreen with delicate but attractive leaves and deep maroon, scented flowers in spring.

Clematis cirrhosa An evergreen clematis with attractive foliage and fragrant cream flowers in late winter and early spring.

***Eccremocarpus scaber* (Chilean glory flower)** This is an evergreen climber with delicate foliage and orange, red or yellow flowers in midsummer. Often grown as an annual in cooler climates.

***Solanum jasminoides* 'Album'**
Evergreen in a sheltered spot, this has pure white potato-like flowers in midsummer and autumn.

***Trachelospermum jasminoides* (star jasmine)** Fragrant white flowers in summer, contrasting with dark evergreen leaves that may take on purplish tints in winter.

Below: *Akebia quinata* has extraordinary maroon flowers set off by delicate, fresh green leaves.

Left: Try an evergreen clematis, such as *C. cirrhosa* var. *balearica*, by the door for winter interest.

white

White flowers offer the perfect contrast with green foliage. They always look clean and bright, especially in the evenings, when they can take on an almost luminous appearance.

play cool by planting...

Clematis armandii 'Snowdrift' An unusual evergreen clematis that has scented white or pinkish flowers in early spring. Prefers a sunny wall or balcony.

Crinum x *powellii* 'Album' Large pure white lily flowers in summer and early autumn. Needs full sun and shelter.

Gaura lindheimeri Delicate white flowers on slender stems. Look out for the variety 'Whirling Butterflies'.

Geranium sanguineum 'Album' This is a superb ground-cover plant with aromatic foliage.

Gypsophila paniculata (baby's breath) Tiny white flowers smother a mass of wiry stems on compact plants.

Helianthemum 'Wisley White' A spreading rock rose for a sunny spot, this has creamy-white flowers with yellow centres.

TIP Deadhead white flowering plants regularly, otherwise the brown faded blooms will distract from the rest of the display

Hydrangea macrophylla 'Lanarth White' This has good foliage, although it is deciduous, and large white lacecap flowers in summer. Growth is pleasingly compact.

Hydrangea petiolaris (climbing hydrangea) A self-clinging climber with attractive leaves and large lace-cap flowers in late summer. The winter bark is also attractive.

Nicotiana sylvestris (tobacco plant) The giant tobacco plant can be perennial in sheltered city areas. Long tubular flowers are sweetly scented in the evening.

Zantedeschia aethiopica 'Crowborough' Dense, lush clumps of long, dark green leaves. White arum-lily like flowers in mid- and late summer. Damp fertile soil in partial shade.

Add some snow-white accents to a planting scheme with *Crinum* x *powellii* 'Album'.

basement

Some of the most interesting 'garden' spaces are those associated with basement living. In close proximity to high walls and often below ground level, these are challenging but ultimately rewarding sites to design, develop, cultivate and enjoy. It's not just a case of adding flowers and foliage. Anything that can be done to provide additional light, colour and interest should be seriously considered.

There was a time when the mention of a basement flat conjured up an image of a cold, dark, dank set of rooms, one step out of the gutter. In the property market, basement flats were considered no better than rabbit holes and the devil's own job to shift. How times have changed. Basement or 'garden' flats are now some of the most desirable properties in larger towns and cities. They regularly command much higher prices than similar accommodation just a few feet higher off the ground. The reason? It's that bit of extra space which so often goes with a basement flat; somewhere outside where there is the chance to flex green fingers and extend the useable living space by creating an outdoor room. A basement area can quickly and easily be turned into a cool, lush enclave for a little relaxation at the end of a hot summer's day in the office.

As larger buildings are being sub-divided into individual dwellings, it's the basement or garden flat that benefits most. The upper floors may be assigned a small section of the original back garden, but who wants a garden that's several flights of stairs away from your home and overlooked by everyone else in the block? On the other hand, the basement flat usually inherits a strip of land that is of no interest to anyone else. It may well be below street level, but it's this that lends it its charm and creates a feeling of enclosure and security. The fact that nobody else should ever need to go down there, means it can also be as private as you want.

There's something rather magical about stepping down into a confined space, a secure area full of foliage and flower. We should view basements as rare and unique planting opportunities. Of course, there is a limit to what can be done, but this can be a godsend, as it quickly indicates exactly what should be done, how, when, where and what with.

With a little thought and planning, the small basement area can become a serviceable garden, full of light, warmth, flower colour and attractive foliage — as interesting as any large acreage, and as enjoyable, too.

A basement area is easily turned into a private and restful outdoor room.

growing environment

Adjacent buildings will have a dramatic effect on growing conditions in and around a basement garden. Understand these and plan and plant accordingly.

shade

The proximity of large structures overshadowing the area mean that natural sunlight is going to be scarce. Although all plants need light to grow, many are perfectly happy in dappled shade. This may well replicate their natural habitats, perhaps in a deciduous wood or on the forest floor. There are even some that seem to require as little light as possible and these are the ones that will thrive in basement borders and planters.

shelter

Being below ground level has its advantages in very windy conditions. We all know how winds get funnelled and deflected around large buildings, increasing in speed and strength as they go. Luckily for us, and our plants, basement areas are naturally sheltered from such extremes. The occasional eddy may decide to stir things

up from time to time, but apart from that and the accompanying deluge of fallen leaves and litter, the basement garden is a sheltered spot and, as such, a favourable place for plants to grow.

temperature

Being predominantly shady means we are dealing with a more even temperature regime in our basement. Towns and cities are also almost always a few degrees warmer than the surrounding countryside. This means that many plants which will not survive in more open suburban gardens just a few miles away will grow quite happily in a city basement garden.

Natural sunlight or sunshine deflected off nearby buildings may strike parts of the garden at

Left: Use mirrors
to reflect available light
and make the area
seem bigger.
Far left: A wall feature
provides a focal
point and occupies very
little space.

Make the most of the moist and sheltered conditions
with a lush selection of foliage plants.

certain times of the day. This can increase temperatures dramatically
and in a short period of time but rarely to the point of damage, as
the effect is short lived.

moisture

The bases of walls are notoriously dry, but the fact that basements
are almost always in permanent shade and protected from drying
winds has beneficial consequences in this respect. Any moisture that
is available stays available to the plants, so subsequent care and
maintenance are reduced. Drainage may be a problem in very wet
weather, although adequate drains should always be present to

prevent flooding in any case. It goes without saying that anything
done in the way of a garden should not interfere with these drains,
or any vents, damp-proof courses, inspection covers or air bricks
associated with the property.

Damp, shady areas where there is little air movement are prone to
getting slippery and this is an important consideration in a basement
garden. Green algae will grow on paving stones or wooden decking,
so make a point of keeping the surfaces clean and safe.

rooms with a view

The view of the basement garden from inside your home is the
most important consideration. If you have little more than people's
ankles and the paws of passing dogs to look at, some strategically
positioned planters can improve the outlook considerably. It will
also give the opportunity to create some degree of privacy, if

necessary: passers by, myself included, often have a passion for peering down into basements to see what's going on there and what's not.

Although the temptation is to erect all manner of trellis screens and rampant climbers, it's also worth remembering that with every inch of window you screen from the road, you're also reducing the same amount of natural light entering your living space. There's a balance to be struck here, and one that can only be achieved through trial, error and some judicious pruning.

Many gardeners would give a lot to have walls around their gardens; the basement gardener is blessed with plenty. The trick is to use these walls to make the most of the available light. For example, a strategically placed mirror can often work wonders. Positioned to one side of the space so it reflects light out of the darkest corners, it's a common design formula that doesn't cost a fortune.

Another excellent idea is to create a focal point, perhaps opposite a window so it can be viewed from inside, too. Simple wall fountains look good and lend themselves to small spaces, adding sound and movement to the overall scheme. With a reasonably large reservoir or tank, they can also be used to grow a collection of bog and marginal plants, which will thrive in the cool, moist conditions. Add trellis or training wires to the remaining walls and you've quadrupled your growing space in just a few hours.

paint

It's also worth experimenting with that other mainstay of the twenty-first century garden – outdoor paint. Paint technology has advanced in recent years and there's now a formulation for every imaginable situation and enough colours to send anyone into a state of apoplexy. Walls, gates and railings can all be transformed with the latest colours. It's always best to limit your colour palette and err on the side of caution. A single bright coloured 'statement' needs a neutral colour to complement it. But if you do make a mistake, it's easily corrected with a coat of something in a more subtle shade.

storage and security

Above all, the basement area needs to be kept serviceable. There will probably be bins, bikes and discarded boots to think about storing, so simplicity is the key. A small, lockable shed or storage box is also a good idea, and can double up as occasional seating, should you be lured outside to relax.

Security is another consideration as basements offer cover for burglars, as well as our chosen plants. Gravel is noisy to walk on, so may deter the opportunist thief. Lights that can be controlled by a movement detector or timer will transform the garden after dark. Many city gardeners are known to potter after dark, even in the depths of winter.

Above: Interesting water plants can be grown in the smallest of bowls.
Left: Use mirrors and other reflective surfaces to increase light in a shady basement.

basement plantings

Due to a lack of sunlight, the mainstay of any basement planting scheme should be dramatic evergreen foliage, and again, less is certainly more, with a few larger plants having a much more impressive effect than a mass (or mess) of smaller ones. A few large planters containing bold evergreen shrubs, bamboos or small trees will provide the main structure, around which smaller, more transient plantings can be created. Bedding plants that are naturally short lived can be used to add flower colour, and bulbs will do particularly well. Because they've made their buds and stored enough food to get growing, even those that prefer bright sunny positions will perform well – although only in their first year.

mirror box

This mirrored planter adds light and a planting opportunity for permanent foliage interest, creating a contemporary feel in a cool, dark basement area.

Interior designers have used mirrors to increase light and hide eyesores for many years. Now mirrors have taken on an architectural role, with reflecting windows camouflaging large buildings and throwing light back into the surrounding neighbourhood. In a basement, these properties can be exploited to make the area seem larger and produce a feeling of light, space and optimism. This simple trough planter could also be used as a free-standing room divider. Large enough to accommodate plants with fairly extensive root systems, it will make a bold statement in a relatively small space, especially when teamed up with a matching wall mirror.

Reflecting all the available light, this mirrored planter will make the most of basement growing conditions.

mirror box

making the planter

It's much easier to make the planter to suit the size of the mirror tiles you buy. This eliminates the need to cut the tiles, and avoids wastage. The box I have used is five tiles long, one high and one wide, producing a planter of pleasing proportions. Scale the basic design to suit your own needs.

you will need:

marine plywood

softwood battens

mirror tiles

waterproof tile adhesive

thick plastic or pond liner

wood screws

wood glue

sticky tape

pencil

tape measure

staple gun

jigsaw

drill

TIP For a firmer fixing, run wood glue along the battens before screwing them to the sides of the box.

1 Measure the mirror tiles, then use their dimensions to mark out the marine plywood, making two sides and two ends that exactly match your chosen number of tiles. Remember to allow for the thickness of the bottom panel of the planter when you measure the sides – when the bottom is attached, the height of the sides should be exactly the height of one tile.

2 Cut battens to fit around the inside of the base of the planter. The bottom panel will be fixed to these. Cut four battens to fit the four corners – remembering to take off the thickness of the bottom batten.

3 Drill pilot holes in the battens to stop them splitting and then attach them to the marine ply panels using wood screws.

4 Measure, cut and attach the bottom panel of the box. Make a few large drainage holes in the base.

5 Line the sides and base of the box with thick plastic or pond liner to protect the wood, stapling it in place, and then make plenty holes in the bottom to allow adequate drainage. A sharp drill will be handy for this.

6 Apply a generous amount of waterproof tile adhesive to the back of the mirror tiles. Carefully stick the tiles to the front of the box, making sure they are aligned properly.

7 Fix mirror tiles to the sides and then use sticky tape to hold them in position just while the glue sets.

planting time

Foliage plants that like a cool, moist environment have been chosen. These are suitable for a shady basement. Most are evergreen, although a few seasonal highlights have been included. Bulbs and bedding plants could also be added.

If possible this planter should be positioned in its final spot before adding the plants. When full of compost and plants and well watered, it will be too heavy to move easily, although it could easily be fitted with wheels.

1 Place a layer of gravel in the bottom of the planter to aid drainage and stop the drainage holes getting clogged up. Add the compost to within 3–4cm (1¼–1½in) of the rim and lightly firm.

2 Water the plants an hour or so before you plant them. Work out what you want to plant where by positioning them on the surface of the compost. Carefully knock the plants out of their pots and check the roots.

3 With the plants in place, back fill around them with more compost – again firming well.

4 Mulch around the plants, taking care to keep the mulch out of the crowns and off the foliage. Water well.

5 The finished planter with background mirror.

TIPS The compost in a large planter will always settle, especially if you don't firm it as you go. This sinkage can sometimes be 5cm (2in) or more. Top up as necessary and if the plants start to look too deep, lift and replant them at the correct level.

For summer nights, consider adding low-voltage spotlights or backlighting for a dramatic effect. Lighting plants close to walls always produces attractive shadows, and with the mirrors also catching the light, the effect would be truly magical.

you will need:

gravel
good quality multi-purpose compost
crushed glass mulch
3 *Blechnum spicant* – evergreen ferns
1 *Carex* 'Silver Sceptre'
1 *Dryopteris wallichiana*
1 *Hosta gracillima* 'Variegata'
1 *Pseudosasa japonica*
1 *Zantedeschia aethiopica* 'Crowborough'

basement plant gallery

foliage

Some of the best plantings are more about foliage than flowers. Where sunlight may be limited to just a couple of hours a day, a basement garden should include a large number of foliage plants.

a few favourites...

Alchemilla mollis (lady's mantle) A perennial with soft downy leaves that catch droplets of water looking like pearls. It bears attractive greenish-yellow flowers in summer.

Griselinia littoralis 'Variegata' This hardy shrub has thick, glossy evergreen leaves with attractive cream and grey variegation.

Heuchera micrantha (coral flower) A spreading perennial with heart-shaped leaves. 'Palace Purple' has metallic bronze-purple leaves.

Hosta fortunei (plantain lily) A super perennial with a wide range of named varieties all having large, attractively marked leaves. 'Aureomarginata' is one of the best with yellow margins.

Pleioblastus auricomus An evergreen bamboo with variegated leaves. Old shoots can be cut out in spring to make room for and expose the brighter new shoots.

Stachys byzantina (lambs' ears) This low-grower has soft woolly, silver leaves and purple flower spikes in summer and early autumn.

ferns

Ferns will love the soft light and moist conditions of the basement, particularly in the summer when more exposed locations quickly become parched and dry.

some of the best...

Adiantum aleuticum 'Japonicum' (northern maidenhair fern) This deciduous fern may be evergreen in sheltered conditions. The new fronds are bronze, turning green as they mature.

Adiantum pedatum A beautiful deciduous fern that thrives in cool, damp conditions.

Blechnum spicant (hard fern) This evergreen fern has lance-shaped, heavily indented leaves, and is ideal for containers in semi-shade. Remove old fronds in spring to allow new ones to unfurl.

Dryopteris erythrosora (Japanese rosy buckler fern) A fern that is evergreen in favourable condi-

tions. When young the triangular fronds are striking coppery-pink, turning light green when mature.

Dryopteris wallichiana (Wallich's wood fern) The deciduous fronds of this fern form a shuttlecock and are yellow-green, contrasting with the almost-black hairs on the midrib.

Polystichum setiferum (soft shield fern) A reliably evergreen fern, forming a rosette of soft, complex, pale green fronds.

> **TIP** All ferns need some care, particularly in the spring. Remove old fronds, even on evergreen varieties, to allow the new ones to develop unhindered.

Right: Ferns of all types will relish the cool, moist shade of a basement garden and associate particularly well with miniature water features.

Below: The dark foliage of *Heuchera micrantha* 'Palace Purple' is ideal for planters in a shady spot.

red

Add some passion to summer pots and containers with fiery red flowers, stems and foliage.

eye-catching top ten...

Acer palmatum 'Corallinum'
A decorative deciduous small tree with new leaves opening a brilliant coral-red in spring.

Cornus alba 'Sibirica' (dogwood)
A deciduous shrub with fine autumn tints and bright red stems in winter.

Crinodendron hookerianum (lantern tree) A large evergreen shrub with lantern-shaped, red flowers from spring to early summer.

Crocosmia 'Bressingham Blaze'
This spreading perennial has attractive deciduous foliage and tubular, orange-red flowers in summer.

Dahlia 'Bishop of Llandaff' This popular dahlia has semi-double flowers held high above deep purple stems and leaves.

Euphorbia griffithii 'Fireglow'
A perennial with evergreen leaves and brilliant red 'flowers', which are actually coloured bracts.

Imperata cylindrica 'Rubra'
A perennial grass with bright red leaves. This spreads but doesn't like cold and wet together so may appreciate a dry winter mulch.

Lychnis chalcedonica (Maltese cross) This perennial has amazingly red flat flowerheads, held high above foliage in early summer.

Rhododendron 'May Day' An evergreen variety with the richest red spring flowers. There are many red rhododendrons to choose from.

Skimmia reevesiana The dark evergreen foliage of this shrub contrasts well with the long-lasting display of red berries in autumn and winter.

Crinodendron hookerianum bears flowers that look like Chinese lanterns in abundant clusters in spring.

step

Inevitably, the smallest spaces offer the biggest challenges, but they're also where the greatest fun can be had. Steps are an ideal place to exercise a little horticultural flair, and can be used to produce some of the most rewarding and eye-catching results. Few garden spaces can be so easily viewed from above and below, so it's a chance to experiment and have some fun.

Wherever you live there are bound to be some steps – just a couple up to a door maybe, or a flight of them traversing a steep change in height or direction. Basement flats are usually blessed with a set, as are roof-top flats, where they allow access or may provide an emergency exit. Wherever they are, such strong architectural elements are a gift for the would-be gardener, offering scope for using a range of climbers and trailers, bedding plants and perennials to create a lush, ever-changing display. It's a chance to experiment with a wide range of pots, containers and all manner of exciting accessories. It's possible to turn something purely functional into a garden space of real beauty.

safety first

Before we do anything else, it is best to consider safety, otherwise that flight of fancy could turn into a flight of fatality. The steps are there for a purpose and anything that hinders their use is potentially dangerous. And just because we know that the plant by the top step has a habit of scratching our ankles, we shouldn't assume that everyone else will be aware of this. Many an unwary visitor has

been attacked by a wayward plant, but if this happens at the top of a flight of steps, it can spell real trouble.

Under the circumstances, common sense should prevail and anything that is likely to cause injury or an accident should be eliminated from our plans right from the start. This obviously rules out plants with thorns or spiny leaves, but should also include anything that will trail or spread too much or that might catch the wind, causing its container to blow over and cascade down the steps.

technically speaking…

It's worth mentioning that the steps themselves may be at fault. Even builders can get it wrong occasionally, producing risers that are too shallow or too high, or making treads that are too small to get a full foot onto or so wide they take a stride or two to master. Steps are for pedestrian traffic and as such they

Right: Wide, shallow steps are the easiest to garden, taking full advantage of the space at the sides.
Far right: Customize tatty steps with tiles or a pebble mosaic.

should work well for the average foot and leg length. If your's are uncomfortable to use, then consider making alterations before placing your first plants. A flight of steps shouldn't rise at an angle greater than 40 degrees. Anything steeper will be difficult to use or unsafe. The risers should be no less than 10cm (4in) high and no greater than 20cm (8in). The treads should be laid at a slight forward angle so rain drains off the front edge of the step.

For aesthetic reasons, and ease of use, the shallower the riser, the deeper the tread should be. Steeper slopes should be traversed in a zigzag fashion with half landings at suitable resting points. For example, a long flight should be broken with a half landing every 10–12 steps.

In step gardening, the width is also of paramount importance as any pots will need space to stand and develop. The would-be gardener with a narrow set of steps should opt for wall-mounted pots and baskets to keep whatever right of way there is useable and free of clutter. Railings can also be used to train and grow plants, and again this keeps the floor space clear, without compromising the horticultural content.

> **TIP** If the steps are less than perfect, a few well-placed and planted containers can help to make them safer. By highlighting the first or last step, or one along the way that's not all it should be, plants can help to slow down foot traffic and draw attention to potential problems.

growing environment

All steps differ in the growing conditions they offer, which can be quite extreme. It pays to check out what sort of problems your plants might have to face before choosing them. Open, metal steps can be cold and windy, while enclosed concrete or brick steps will be sheltered and either cold or warm. Light can be a problem, especially in confined areas, such as stairwells and side entrances. All the plants you choose will have to be happy in containers and the containers themselves will inevitably have to be on the small side. Plants able to cope with occasional drought and a limited root run will do best and should be top of the shopping list.

Above: The wider the tread, the shallower the riser should be.
Right: The confined space of a flight of steps produces its own microclimate.

planning a display

Of all the areas around the home, steps are the most fun to plan and plant. They can be viewed from different angles and provide instant height or depth, which means the planting can be varied and entertaining. An overall theme is always a good idea. This is a trick that professional designers use in both gardens and interior schemes. By using one recurring element, perhaps a colour or material, you can draw together a scheme that is already coping with a less than ideal environment. The same is true of steps, where a set of matching pots, a linking colour or a repeated plant will go a long way towards producing a cohesive and attractive display.

Although it is tempting to grow a wide range of plants, with steps, simplicity is the key, and a limited planting palette will pay dividends. Similar plants with similar likes and dislikes will be easier to look after, although any differences in their growth or flowering ability will be that bit more noticeable. I always recommend neat compact plants that are less likely to get damaged, and choose containers that are decorative from all angles, so when the display is viewed straight on or from below there is still something attractive to look at.

The display itself can be changed at will, perhaps moving plants from the shady steps to the sunny ones so more even growth is maintained. The plants will also need turning occasionally so they don't become lopsided. And with such a small place to plant, a bit of extravagance can be forgiven, so it's worth considering a changing seasonal display, which can work particularly well. Replacing all the plants for spring, summer, autumn and winter can become expensive, but if it's all we have to do, then why not? A vibrant mix of tender summer bedding can be quickly transformed into an autumn mix of grasses and bulbs, changed again for winter evergreens and berries, and then again in spring for a jewel box of primulas and dwarf bulbs.

step dressings

Don't forget that the steps can be given a bit of a facelift – unattractive concrete or paving can be painted, decked, tiled or covered with metal – so they become a decorative part of the overall scheme. Again, making sure they aren't made slippery or unsafe. It's another chance to personalize a space, which is what gardening is all about.

Accessories can also be used to enhance the display – a collection of pebbles, perhaps, or some attractive driftwood or outdoor candles. Such displays are easy to change as styles and personal preference dictate, or as the seasons pass by. Anything can be used to enhance a theme so long as it doesn't interfere with the use of the steps and will not blow away or down.

one step at a time

Turn the pots into a living piece of art. With just a short flight of steps there is the chance to create something really special.

All the best garden designers include an element of repetition in their designs – a plant, colour, structure or shape that recurs around a garden brings an element of cohesiveness to the overall design. By placing identical pots or plantings on each step, we can do the same. But a series of identical pots all containing the same plants could look pretty boring and would also highlight any plant that refused to grow as strongly as the rest, which is almost inevitable in gardening. So how about varying the plants you use or decorating each of the pots slightly differently so they have an overall co-ordinating theme but are also individual?

1 Make sure the pots are completely clean. An old pot may benefit from a wash with a weak bleach solution to kill off any algae that would affect the paint. Apply a thick base coat of exterior paint with a brush. This base coat will give the pots a uniform appearance and highlight the subsequent colours. Leave to dry.

2 Spray on patterns in the colours of your choice. You can work freehand to create a 'graffiti' effect or use a straight edge to create soft lines. Leave the pot to dry thoroughly before planting. A sealing coat of matt yacht varnish may help pots survive extreme winter weather.

3 Put crocks in the bottom of the pot, before carefully placing the plant in the pot, taking care not to damage the roots or mark the leaves. I've used a thick, fleshy-leafed sempervivum as it will stay compact and relish the warm, sheltered, free-draining conditions.

you will need:

plants of your choice – alpines and
    succulents work well

terracotta pots

exterior wall or terracotta paint

exterior spray paints – a selection
    of colours

wood offcut

gravel or crocks

multi-purpose compost

decorative mulch

paint brushes

newspaper

4 Mulch around the top of the pot to keep the leaves and neck of the plant off the compost and display the plant to its best advantage.

5 Dressed with a few shells and arranged on the steps, the plants and pots will look attractive from any viewpoint.

plants used here include...

Buxus sempervirens (box)

Carex 'Silver Sceptre'

Dryopteris wallichiana (buckler fern)

Euphorbia viguerii

Changing light and shadows will help
to show the pots and plants off to
their full advantage.

step plant gallery

herbs

For colour, scent and culinary use some container-grown herbs are a useful addition to the planting mix. Most like a warm spot and free-draining compost. On a flight of steps, they'll release their scent every time someone brushes past them.

look out for...

Chamomile *(Chamaemelum nobile)*
A carpeting plant with fine, ferny foliage and small white daisy flowers.

Chives *(Allium schoenoprasum)*
Attractive grass-like, deep green leaves and typically mauve onion-type flowers.

Feverfew *(Tanacetum parthenium)*
Bright green foliage and masses of small white daisy flowers with yellow centres.

Mint *(Mentha)* There is a wide range of smells and flavours to choose from. Try the sweet applemint *(M. suaveolens)*, traditional spearmint *(M. spicata)*, ginger mint *(M. x gentilis* 'Variegata' or lemon balm *(M. officinalis)*. All can be invasive so pot culture is ideal.

Parsley *(Petroselinum crispum)* The frilly green leaves make this herb ideal to be used as an ornamental plant. Cut out flowering shoots to maintain the supply of fresh leaves.

> **TIP** In the winter bring a few pots indoors and place them on a windowsill so they continue to grow and provide fresh, aromatic foliage.

other herbs include...

Bay *(Laurus nobilis)*
Bergamot *(Monarda didyma)*
Borage *(Borago officinalis)*
Coriander *(Coriandrum sativum)*
Cotton lavender *(Santolina chamaecyparissus)*
Dill *(Anethum graveolens)*
French tarragon *(Artemisia dracunculus)*
Ginger *(Zingiber officinale)*
Lavender *(Lavandula angustifolia)*
Lemon balm *(Melissa officinalis)*
Lemon verbena *(Aloysia triphylla)*
Marigold *(Calendula officinalis)*
Rosemary *(Rosmarinum officinalis)*
Sage *(Salvia officinalis)*
Sweet cicely *(Myrrhis odorata)*
Thyme *(Thymus vulgaris)*
Winter savory *(Satureja montana)*

annuals

Whether bought as seeds, seedlings or plants, annuals are hard to beat for instant colour. Easily planted among existing shrubs and through ground-cover, they're a chance to change the look of a planting without major upheaval.

hardy annuals...

These don't need nurturing on a windowsill or in a greenhouse.

Agrostemma githago (corn cockle) Grey-green leaves with magenta flowers. Thrives on poor soil in full sun. Great for bees.

Anchusa capensis (alkanet) Hairy leaves set off bright blue flowers with a white eye. Look out for the more compact variety 'Blue Angel'.

Borago officinalis (borage) Bristly leaves and stems are decorated with bright blue flowers all summer. Makes a large plant.

Calendula officinalis (marigold) Single or double, daisy-like flowers in shades of cream, yellow and orange. Good for cutting and adding to salads and soups.

Centaurea cyanus (cornflower) Typical cornflowers in red, pink or white.

Clarkia amoena (godetia, satin flower) Frilled, single or double flowers that prefer slight shade.

Collinsia bicolor (Chinese houses) A weak-stemmed but prolific flowering addition to containers with flowers in shades of white, pink and lilac.

Consolida ajacis (larkspur) This is like a miniature delphinium, with

flowers in shades of white, pink, blue and mauve. Well worth growing.

Cynoglossum amabile (Chinese forget-me-not, hound's tongue) Hairy leaves and sky-blue flowers.

Eschscholzia californica (California poppy) Fine, feathery foliage and tissue paper poppy flowers. Usually orange but new varieties include pinks, white, yellow and cream. Superb on poor soil in full sun.

Gypsophila elegans (baby's breath) This is a wonderful filler plant, its filigree stems dusted with small, white or pale pink flowers. Excellent for cutting.

Limnanthes douglasii (poached egg plant) A spreading edging plant with cup-shaped flowers, yellow in the centre with white edges. They produce plenty of nectar, which attracts beneficial bees and hoverflies.

Linaria maroccana (toadflax) This is a rather lax grower but varieties offer snapdragon-like flowers in every colour of the spectrum.

Linum grandiflorum (flowering flax) A slender plant with saucer-shaped flowers that may be white, rose-pink or purple, depending on the variety.

Malcomia maritima (Virginian stock) Sweetly fragrant flowers in white, pink or purple. Early sowing will produce a better display if the summer turns out hot and humid.

Malope trifida (annual mallow) This plant has flowers veined with a darker colour. It is tall and free flowering from summer into autumn. Will self-seed.

Papaver rhoeas (Flanders poppy) Downy foliage and tissue paper-thin poppy flowers. Look out for the mixtures and blends in subtle shades of pink, peach, mauve, red and white.

Papaver somniferum (opium poppy) This poppy has blue-green, fleshy leaves and large single or double, bowl-shaped flowers. The seedheads are attractive, too.

Phacelia campanularia (Californian bluebell) Hairy leaves and upturned bell-shaped flowers in bright blue, occasionally white.

Scabiosa atropurpurea (pincushion flower, scabious) Wiry stems bear rosette flowers in white, pale blue and mauve. Many interesting varieties.

perennials

Many people think that perennials are the preserve of the garden border. They're not. Lots positively thrive in containers, where they're free from the competition of other plants and can be admired in all their intricate detail.

will not disappoint...

Agapanthus **(African lily)** Large strap-shaped leaves and large blue or white flowers. Look out for the varieties 'Headbourne hybrids' and 'Bressingham White'.

Argyranthemum This plant needs winter protection and so is often grown as an annual. It has clear, white or yellow daisy flowers with a bright yellow eyes. 'Jamaica Primrose' is one of the best with larger yellow flowers.

Diascia rigescens An attractive trailing plant with delicate pink flowers in summer.

Hedychium gardnerianum **(ginger lily)** Large leaves and fragrant flowers in summer and early autumn. A real feature plant, it may appreciate some winter protection.

Hosta **(plantain lily)** All hostas have architectural leaves – in a multitude of shapes, sizes and colours, depending on the variety. They are best grown in pots so are ideal for steps, where slugs and snails will have more of a job reaching them.

Pelargonium **(geranium)** Geraniums are usually grown as annuals or protected over winter indoors. They have fleshy leaves and spectacular flowers in shades of white, red, pink and mauve. Look out for scented-leafed

varieties for additional interest. Trailing ivy-leafed geraniums are also well suited to steps, balconies and hanging baskets.

Penstemon These have attractive tubular flowers in mid- to late summer. The plants are susceptible to frost so tend to die back and

sprout from the base the following spring.

Tolmiea menziesii **(piggyback plant)** A superb perennial, grown for its attractive foliage, which may be evergreen in favoured conditions. Young plants form on top of the mature leaves.

Above: Everyone's favourite foliage plant, the plantain lily (*Hosta*). This is the ever-popular 'Francis Williams'. Top left: For poor soil in a sunny spot, try the Californian poppy (*Eschscholzia californica*). This is the aptly named variety 'Inferno'.
Far left: Lemon-scented balm (*Melissa officinalis*) has one of the strongest and freshest foliage scents.

orange

Adding a contemporary look to any planting, orange flowers lift the spirits, and they contrast well with dark foliage.

my top ten...

Campsis x *tagliabuana* '**Madame Galen**' A superb, exotic-looking climber with large, orange, trumpet-shaped flowers in summer and early autumn.

Canna '**Striata**' A hybrid with bright orange flowers that complement the purple stems and vivid green leaves in summer and early autumn.

Eccremocarpus scaber (**Chilean glory flower**) A lovely evergreen climber with orange-red flowers from spring to autumn.

Euphorbia mellifera (**honey spurge**) A shrub with evergreen leaves and rich orange, honey-scented flowers.

Fritillaria imperialis (**crown imperial**) This bulb has large fleshy rosettes of leaf, high above which are produced spectacular orange, bell-shaped flowers.

Fuchsia '**Thalia**' A vigorous variety with long tubular, orange-red flowers.

Geum coccineum This perennial has attractive foliage and bright orange flowers with yellow centres held on long stems. 'Prince of Orange' and 'Tangerine' are two others to try.

Helianthemum '**Fire Dragon**' A bright orange-red rock rose with silvery-grey leaves, ideal for a sunny spot.

Iris foetidissima (**stinking iris**) Well worth growing for the bright orange seeds that erupt out of the seed pods in autumn, this iris also has the bonus of attractive evergreen leaves.

Rosa '**Buff Beauty**' This rose has new coppery brown foliage, followed by richly scented, double, orange flowers.

Few bulbs can beat the crown imperial (*Fritillaria imperialis*) for impact. This is the superb orange variety 'The Premier'.

yard

The courtyard is often as close to a garden as we can get, but it's still full of possibilities and promise.

Any outdoor space has the potential to be a garden, even if it's completely surrounded by high walls and receives very little natural daylight. Courtyards, or backyards, are often described as 'offering potential' when a property is on the market, but too few are ever put to good use. Despite the best of intentions, they very often become a dumping ground for bikes, ladders and unwanted furniture, and that 'potential' is never realized. Perhaps it's because people tend to think that if there's no soil, limited light and broken concrete all over the base, creating a garden is out of the question or would cost a fortune. Nothing could be further from the truth. With a little ingenuity, a modicum of planning, an eye for detail and some enthusiasm, a boring concrete area can be turned into a miniature courtyard with all the charm of a much larger, traditional garden space.

identify the space

In buildings that have been converted into flats, ground floor properties are very often sold with the original garden, or at least a section of it. In purpose-built blocks, this is rarely the case, as the builders will have made maximum use of the space available and built as close to the site's boundaries as they dare. However, very often, even this sort of site will have areas that it's not feasible to develop and these are usually apportioned to one of the ground floor properties to ensure that someone is responsible for their upkeep. A property that

includes a small outside area offers plenty of scope to exercise a growing passion. Of all the areas around a gardenless home, the courtyard is probably the one that provides the most opportunities. It's the perfect place to practice some horticultural expertise.

get the inspiration

Some of the most enchanting gardens have been created in courtyards. Visit any major city, particularly in Europe, and step off the main tourist trails and very soon you discover minute spaces, squeezed in between existing buildings, that have been turned into gorgeous garden rooms. These courtyards may be used for outdoor living and entertaining, or they may simply be planted and groomed so they provide otherwise viewless windows and doors with an attractive outlook. They may be so small that there's no room even for a chair, but a carefully positioned pot of plants can easily be enjoyed when glimpsed through a window or an open door.

On a larger scale, the grand designers of yesteryear who had huge estates to develop, included formal, enclosed gardens in their plans, but they had to go to the trouble of building walls and planting hedges to achieve the desired effect. It is possible to borrow ideas from these large courtyards and scale them down to suit our own needs, style and budget.

Make full use of walls to add colour and act as a display area for treasured possessions.

growing environment

We've already seen how the conditions vary around different parts of the house. In the courtyard, aspect and the prevailing winds play their part, but adjacent buildings provide the necessary shelter and enclosure. Also, on the plus side, the walls and fences offer a pleasing backdrop as well as valuable protection to choice, tender or unusual plants

On the minus side, there may be relatively low light levels and no direct sunshine at all. Flowers may find it difficult to thrive in such circumstances, but all manner of foliage plants will revel in them. The trick is to capitalize on the shady conditions and use plants that are more naturally at home in woodland areas.

Many garden gardeners would kill for such a planting opportunity as they battle with sharp frosts, strong winds and baking hot sunshine. The courtyard will be sheltered from such extremes and, as such, is a reasonably controlled planting environment. Like the basement, this is a unique microclimate, quite different from traditional gardens just a stone's throw away.

making a choice

All we need to do is assess the situation and decide what ambience we wish to create. In a small space it perhaps seems odd to recommend large plants, but it really is the simplest and quickest way of creating a dramatic effect along with plenty of visual interest. Lots of tiny, almost apologetic pots, clustered to one side of a door, will take quite a bit of looking after but add little in the way of impact or form. However, a large container planted with one major shrub, small multi-stemmed tree or bamboo will create just the right atmosphere in the same situation and it will add enough structure to deserve being allocated such an important position. So long as it's possible to get it home, and through the flat into the courtyard once there, then it's well worth considering. Splashing out on a couple of expensive plants can be seen as an investment for the future. Being potted, they can be moved as easily as a piece of furniture, so when it's time to move house the plants can go too. Planted out in a new garden, they'll soon realise they can grow more vigorously and reach their full potential.

Large plants can be trained and clipped into decorative shapes. For example, the art of cloud pruning, in which evergreen plants are encouraged to produce long branches with blobs of greenery at the ends, has become popular. Mature specimens are expensive but worth the price, unless you're prepared to wait 10–20 years to achieve the effect yourself. Alternatively, try more traditional topiary shapes, which are fun to create and add all-year-round interest.

There's always the chance of growing something more exotic, although where the plant is going to go in the winter should be considered at the time of buying. Tree ferns from Australia and New Zealand would be perfect, enjoying shady but moist conditions and forming a strong visual impact with their hairy brown trunks and splayed green fronds. With some protection, they'll survive winter outdoors in most areas.

But the planting doesn't have to stop with one or two large plants. Making the most of the space, we should aim to layer the plants in each

It doesn't take much to turn an unpromising backyard into a beautiful courtyard garden.

container and plan a continuity of interest right through the year. Strangely enough, it's in winter, when we're more likely to be housebound, that the yard will become more important to us, so planning some winter interest is imperative. Traditional winter bedding and berrying shrubs are a good start, with early, mid- and late spring bulbs bringing up the rear.

Aim to include perennials, annuals, summer bulbs and a few trailing plants in each pot to make the most of the opportunity presented to us. With so many plants vying for the same patch of compost, they'll need much more attention than your average pot plant, but with such a small space to look after, this is hardly going to tax the caretaker.

down to earth

The best way to start is to clear the area completely, and brush down the walls and floor to see what's what. Even the most neglected courtyard will be transformed if it's cleared of all its debris and given a bit of a tidy up. The area will also seem larger. It is also at this point that we may discover that it could best be described as 'offering considerable scope for improvement', but this doesn't mean

Left: Use salvaged items to add character and personality.

Right: Tender exotics, such as this beautiful but poisonous *Ricinus gibsonii*, will revel in the warm, sheltered environment of a courtyard.

it's time to give up – quite the contrary. Repointing, rendering or painting walls is now a simple DIY task, as is putting trellis panels on the walls if a big cover-up is necessary.

Judging how much should be done on a structural level depends on your terms of occupancy. Owner-occupiers will obviously be more inclined to spend time and money putting things right, such as mending broken windows, sorting out the flooring and drainage, painting walls and even installing lights. It's an investment for the future with the added bonus of enjoyment during the intervening years. Tenants should consult their landlord or letting agents to see what the owner is prepared to do. With someone who's showing an interest in improving the property, landlords are often more inclined to contribute to the costs involved. However, this is not always the case, with some landlords showing even less inclination to spend money on the surroundings than they do on the property itself. If little support is forthcoming then a cosmetic approach can be taken, doing just enough to make it presentable but without spending a fortune that will ultimately benefit someone else. This way the space can be used and appreciated as part of the home rather than being a constant bugbear.

using the space

First and foremost we need to bear in mind that the courtyard has to fulfil a number of roles. There's no point creating a garden there if it's going to be in the way. Undoubtedly, access to and from the property will be required. The area may also have to allow communal access or provide an escape route in the event of an emergency: it's particularly vital to check that it's not a recognized fire exit, although this should have been highlighted in the property searches or as part of the tenancy agreement.

Second, the area may have to be used for other things. Small, city flats are often cramped and everyone knows that modern day life involves a fair amount of ancillary equipment. Bikes are a good example; they can't be left on the street, so the courtyard may have to perform a storage role. Clothes also need somewhere to dry, so it may be necessary to incorporate a clothesline into your plans. In the interests of efficiency, most of the utility companies now install meters on the outside of properties and these will need reading from time to time. Allowing free access to the meters is a necessary evil, although they can easily be disguised in a cupboard or behind a plant.

Take all these needs into consideration, and add the fact that it would be quite nice to be able to sit out there from time to time, and

it becomes obvious that the smaller the space, the more multi-functional it needs to be.

Next, it's a good idea to look at the courtyard from inside. Unlike those people who look out onto a street or car park, if you are blessed with an enclosed space you can do something to improve your view. The rooms that overlook the area may also influence its design, perhaps enhance an interior theme.

making a start

A simple plan on paper is a good starting point; if it can be drawn to scale so much the better. Plotting the position of doors and windows will help you decide where planters are best placed and where to position the all-important focal point. Making mistakes on paper is a lot less expensive and exasperating than doing them for real.

Any good garden designer starts by plotting the immovable objects around which the design and planting must evolve. On a large scale, this includes the house, large trees and any major features that are to be retained. With a courtyard, it can be scaled down, with important items including doors, windows, gates, inspection covers and any drainage pipes, drains, air bricks and vents. Once you have identified these as a framework, plants and materials can be used to hide or disguise them while also enhancing the space.

floors

In the home, the foundation for any room is a good floor, and in a courtyard the base material is just as important. Work with what's there or change it: the choice is ours. Bearing in mind that nothing should impede any existing drains and air vents. It is also vital not to bridge the building's damp-proof course. This can be identified by a thicker line of mortar between the bricks just above ground level, through which an impermeable membrane is laid to prevent moisture from the soil and foundations seeping up the walls. On rendered walls, it's more difficult to see, so advice from a builder or surveyor may be required.

Invariably, little attention has been paid to the base of small courtyards: at best there may be some paving slabs, at worst nothing at all. In fact, it is better if there isn't a hard surface, because this means there is the option of improving the soil and planting directly into the ground, then simply surfacing the amount of ground that we want to. Of course the soil will need improving but the effort is well worth it.

As far as hard surfacing is concerned, the owner-occupier has the advantage of doing exactly as they choose. Such a small but valuable space can be treated to an expensive surface like natural stone, block paving or ceramic tiles. The size of the area involved means that the expense is minimal and, in any case, the aesthetic value and longevity

of top quality materials will be adequate compensation for any money you have to spend.

The tenant, on the other hand, needs to consider the cost more carefully and may have to opt for a more cosmetic change. Even cleaning up what's there with a proprietary patio cleaner or pressure washer can smarten up the most unpromising material. Alternatively, a layer of gravel or shingle, wooden decking, even synthetic grass, can be laid over the existing surface with the minimum of fuss and upheaval.

walls and fences

These are the key to making the most of the available space, and can be painted to suit individual tastes. Exterior masonry paints and wood treatments are now available in any colour or finish we could desire. Tiling the walls is also an option, as is using willow or bamboo screens for a country or oriental effect (see also Wall, pp.76–87).

Wall pots, hanging baskets and planters all provide additional growing space without taking up any room at all. However, fences will need to be secure and sturdy enough to take their weight, which can be considerable. Alternatively, if things are looking a little fragile, climbers can easily be planted in pots on the ground and encouraged up training wires or trellis panels. They'll soon clothe the fence or wall with foliage and flowers.

Left: In a small space it is more affordable to use quality materials such as wood, stone and stainless steel.
Right: The smallest space can be used to house a personal collection of plants, often subjects that are a little tender and prefer the shelter of adjacent walls.

> **THAT PERENNIAL PROBLEM – STORAGE** There's absolutely no reason why storage can't be provided in an attractive and unobtrusive way. There are plenty of neat corner sheds and storage boxes on the market that can hide any amount of junk. Or why not use storage chests as occasional seating or a platform to display a collection of potted plants? Alternatively, try making a feature of the items to be stored. A trendy bike can be mounted on the wall alongside the windsurfer, so they performing a garden art role while you are taking things a little easier. And remember shelves look great outside and can double up as storage and a display stand for small and trailing potted plants.

focal points

For a focal point, consider any traditional garden element that is tall but on the thin side. The most obvious is the obelisk, either as a purely decorative element or as a climbing frame for more plants. Wire, stone, glass, wood, trellis or even mirrored, the obelisk adds permanent structure and interest, regardless of whether it's covered with plants or not. Painted a vibrant colour or designed to tone in with its surroundings, it will make a statement and draw the eye – the perfect focal point.

Simpler, but no less attractive is a post, again either used to support a climber or simply as a structural element. Put several in a row and you have the makings of a pergola, perhaps with the cross beams supported by an adjacent wall producing a cloister effect.

seating and storage

Some form of seating is essential if the courtyard is big enough, and there's something extremely satisfying about being able to sit outside when it's raining and not get wet. A covered seat or arbour is the simplest way of achieving this. Again, it can be painted and decorated to individual tastes and also used to support climbing plants. Doubling up a seat as a storage area and a focal point is even better. In fact, tables and chairs need careful consideration and in all but the largest courtyards may not be a viable option. Choosing furniture for the dining room or kitchen that can also be taken outside works well, doing away with the problem of storage.

Use a canvas or sailcloth canopy to create shelter and shade and add colour and interest. Old windsurfer sails in jewel colours can brighten up the dullest corner and the board itself can be propped against the wall as another focal point.

reflect on this

An idea that crops up regularly around the home is the use of a mirror to make a space seem larger. Mirrors can also be positioned to make the most of available light. These characteristics can be employed to good effect in even the smallest of courtyards. For example, if your space is so narrow that, from the window, it's impossible to see what's planted outside, position a mirror opposite and angle it down towards the plants to bring them back into view. Mirrors can be framed with trellis to create an impression of a garden beyond or to widen narrow spaces and lengthen short ones. However they're used, make sure the mirror is suitable for a damp environment and is securely attached to the wall.

finding the source

Garden centres, garden ornament suppliers and architectural salvage and reclamation yards are all good hunting grounds for interesting garden features. Very often something with a totally different original intention can be pressed into service as a garden feature. Old terracotta chimney pots are a good example: they are ideal for raised plantings of trailing plants. Old ladders could be propped against a wall and used to hang baskets from or train climbers up. Old lamps, perhaps with very decorative standards, are also an interesting idea. Decorative in themselves, they can also perform a functional role if a power supply can be arranged and then the courtyard can be used and enjoyed after dark.

a carpet of bricks

This is a simple concept that costs very little to achieve, is strangely satisfying and will always provoke discussion among friends and neighbours.

Create an intricate, yet simple planting area, using basic bricks or blocks laid in a geometric pattern. The blocks are contained in a frame and can be moved around to suit different looks and moods and spaces can be left for simple 'carpet bedding' planting. The area can be walked over, changed at will and provides a cosmetic solution to a perennial problem – hiding anything unsightly on the ground, such a drains or manholes, but still allowing access to them. It's an idea that would work equally well on a balcony or roof terrace.

Avoid having to cut blocks, which can be time-consuming and wasteful, by measuring them and calculating a convenient size for the finished carpet.

you will need:

paving bricks
wood battens
wood screws
wood glue
sharp sand

exterior woodstain
saw
drill
paint brushes
newspaper
rake

good ground-cover plants to try include...

Ajuga reptans 'Multicolor'
Chamomile
Heuchera micrantha 'Palace Purple'
Lysimachia nummularia
Sedum acre
Thyme

add some colour...

With so many good floor and exterior stone paints available why not customize the blocks and produce a Persian carpet from plants? Coloured blocks can also be moved around to form different patterns.

1 Make up a frame from the wooden battens. Gluing and screwing the corner joint will make them more rigid. Paint the frame in a colour that complements or contrasts with the bricks you have chosen.

2 Position the frame where you want the carpet to be and fill it with a layer of sharp sand to facilitate better drainage. The sand layer also provides a good bed for the blocks and will sort out any slight unevenness in the base below.

3 Rake the sand level and start positioning the blocks in the pattern of your choice.

4 Leave gaps for plants, a collection of stones, a piece of turf or a miniature plantscape. It's also a good way of making a temporary planter for succulents, which will relish a summer outside in the sun.

yard plant gallery

evergreens

In a small courtyard, evergreens will provide permanent interest and a suitable backdrop for more seasonal planting schemes. Large evergreen shrubs can also be used to screen unsightly pipes or storage areas.

eight to consider...

Aucuba japonica (Japanese laurel) This is the perfect container evergreen. It has large, deep green leaves and responds well to pruning if it gets too big. 'Crotonifolia' has leaves spotted and splashed with yellow.

Berberis thunbergii This shrub has prickly stems with rounded leaves in shades of green, red or gold, depending on the variety. Flowers are followed by a good display of berries. A favourite is 'Golden Ring', which has yellow-edged, purple leaves that turn red in autumn.

Camellia japonica (camellia) The well-known camellia has glossy leaves and magnificent single or double flowers in a wide range of colours, depending on the variety.

Daphne odora 'Aureo-marginata' A superb shrub with yellow-edged leaves and beautifully fragrant winter flowers.

Elaeagnus x *ebbingei* This shrub as glossy green leaves on sturdy stems. Look out for the variety 'Limelight', which has leaves marked with yellow and pale green in the centres. 'Gilt Edge' has yellow margins.

For evergreen interest, look no further than *Elaeagnus* x *ebbingei* 'Limelight'.

Erica arborea 'Estrella Gold' (tree heather) Lime-green foliage is tipped with yellow on this upright shrub. In late spring, it is smothered in white flowers.

Gaultheria procumbens (checker-berry, wintergreen) A superb ground-cover plant with purple autumn foliage tints and bright red berries. Both the berries and the leaves are aromatic.

Pittosporum tenuifolium (kohuhu) This tree has glossy leaves with frilly edges. Look out for coloured-leaved forms, such as red-brown 'Tom Thumb', mottled white and green 'Irene Patterson' and yellow 'Golden King'.

ground-cover

The lack of a traditional flowerbed doesn't mean interesting ground-cover plants can't be used. They add to the overall display and also helping to conserve moisture and keep down weeds.

The glossy, evergreen leaves of *Ajuga reptans* 'Catlin's Giant'.

my favourites include...

Ajuga reptans 'Catlin's Giant' An effective ground-cover with decorative evergreen leaves. Short spikes of blue flowers are displayed in early summer.

Bergenia 'Silberlicht' This is a spring-flowering hardy perennial, displaying white, bell-like flowers backed by large, heart-shaped evergreen leaves.

Cardamine trifoliatum An evergreen perennial with dark green, rounded, toothed leaves in three parts. Small, conspicuous white flowers in spring.

Epimedium grandiflorum (barrenwort) This low-grower has evergreen heart-shaped leaves and attractive flowers in late spring. 'Rose Queen' has bronze leaves. 'White Queen' has white flowers.

Pratia pedunculata 'County Park' A small, vigorous carpeting plant spangled with rich blue-violet, starry flowers. Perfect for bed edges, rock gardens, cracks in old paving, tubs, troughs and containers.

Pratia treadwellii An alpine ground-cover plant, producing a mass of small white, star-shaped flowers – unfortunately, slugs also seem to like the flowers.

Salix reticulata A spreading willow with rough-textured, oval leaves, paler beneath. Male plants produce catkins in spring.

Soleirolia soleirolii (helxine) An invasive mossy plant with minute leaves held close to the ground. Excellent for carpeting in troughs and around containers. Likes damp shade.

Thymus vulgaris (thyme) All the thymes make good ground-cover, with the added bonus of flowers and scent. 'Aureus' is silver-leaved while 'Silver Posie' has white-edged leaves.

exotic

Lush, exotic planting is always fashionable and a good way of linking the indoors with an outside space. Many more tender plants will survive the winter in towns and cities, but would fail in the colder, more exposed countryside. It's possible to grow a wide range of exotic, or exotic-looking, plants in pots and containers.

a dozen to look for...

Aralia elata (Japanese angelica) A vigorous tree with attractive foliage, especially in the form 'Variegata'.

Catalpa bignonioides (Indian bean tree) A spreading tree with large leaves. Look out for the golden-leaved form 'Aurea'.

Chamaerops humilis (dwarf fan palm) Spectacular fan-shaped leaves; occasional yellow flowers.

Cordyline australis (New Zealand cabbage palm) This plant produces a woody stem on top of which is a rosette of thick, strap-shaped leaves. The leaves of 'Purple Tower' are flushed with purple, while those of 'Torbay Dazzler' are cream striped and margined. A good feature plant.

Cycas revoluta (sago palm) One to stand out in the summer with stiff, fern-like leaves growing from a central trunk. Slow growing.

Dicksonia antarctica (tree fern) This fern has magnificent leaves radiating from the top of a central stem. Needs frost protection and plenty of water in summer.

Eucalyptus gunnii (cider gum) One of many attractive eucalyptus' with silvery, aromatic leaves and decorative bark. Eucalyptus' can be hard-pruned to keep them within bounds.

Above: *Cycas revoluta* has distinctive arching and leathery leaves.
Left: The golden form of the Indian bean tree (*Catalpa bignonioides* 'Aurea').

Fatsia japonica Large evergreen leaves are the main feature of this plant, which also produces cream flowers and black berry-like fruits.

Lonicera hildebrandiana An evergreen climbing honeysuckle with huge cream and gold, fragrant flowers in summer. The leaves are rounded, glossy and fresh apple-green. Needs a warm position or grow it in a conservatory.

Melianthus major Large, toothed, grey-green leaves are produced on a spreading shrub.

Phormium tenax (New Zealand flax) Rigid, upright, strap-shaped leaves with occasional, long-lasting flowers. Look for the bronze 'Aurora' with red stripes, the orange, red and pink 'Dazzler', and 'Sundowner', the best for a combination of green with pink margins.

Yucca filamentosa (Adam's needle) Long, thick, pointed leaves from a central rosette. 'Variegata' has blue-green leaves edged with white. 'Bright Edge' has yellow leaf margins.

TIP If you decide to buy a tender specimen plant, remember that it may have to come indoors for the winter, so make sure that you have somewhere to put it.

shrubs

Shrubs should do more than just sit there. Correctly chosen, they can provide interest all year round, with spring flowers, summer fruits and autumn tints. They can also be used to support annual and perennial climbers.

value for money...

Clerodendron trichotomum (glory tree) A deciduous shrub with large leaves, this bears delicate sprays of fragrant white flowers in late summer and autumn berries.

Desfontania spinosa A prickly evergreen with unusual orange and red, tubular flowers from summer through to late autumn.

Lavatera 'Rosea' (tree mallow) A vigorous, semi-evergreen shrub, producing large sprays of soft pink, funnel-shaped flowers in summer and autumn.

Magnolia liliflora A deciduous shrub with goblet-shaped, deep red flowers in spring before the leaves. 'Nigra' is a compact form that flowers well when still quite young.

Philadelphus 'Belle Etoile' (mock orange) Deciduous with dark green leaves and a mass of richly fragrant, single white flowers in late spring and early summer.

Photinia glabra 'Rubens' An evergreen with long, thin, glossy leaves and spectacular red new shoots in spring.

Pieris japonica This has glossy evergreen leaves, white flowers and vibrant red new shoots in spring.

Viburnum plicatum (Japanese snowball bush) A deciduous shrub with deep green leaves and flat heads of white flowers. Good autumn colour. The varieties 'Lanarth', 'Grandiflorum' and 'Mariesii' are particularly good.

Weigela 'Looymansii Aurea' A spreading, deciduous shrub with yellow leaves and pink tubular flowers in early summer.

> **TIP** Large containers necessary for trees will take up valuable space, but they can also be planted with some decorative ground-cover, and you might find that the shade from the tree means there's no need for an umbrella. Look for plants that have been trained as multi-stemmed specimens as they're less likely to grow as large and they'll provide more bark and structural interest at a lower level.

trees

In a small courtyard, large balcony or roof terrace, a tree can add interest, structure and much needed shade. Planted in large containers of good quality compost they'll be perfectly happy but will need regular feeds and careful watering for the rest of their lives.

ten to try...

Acer palmatum 'Sango-kaku' An all-year-round tree with bright coral-pink winter stems and attractive leaves that open a shade of orange and turn pale yellow in winter.

Amelanchier canadensis This has white flowers and pink-tinted new leaves in spring, purple berries in summer and spectacular autumn colour. *A. laevis* has even better autumn colour. Prefers full sun but copes with partial shade.

Betula utilis 'Jacquemontii' This birch will grow to 10m (30ft) but multi-stemmed specimens will stay smaller. It can also be pruned. Trim off the lower branches to expose the bark. The white stems look best in winter.

Cornus kousa var. chinensis A slow-growing but spectacular tree with white bracts in spring that turn pink by summer. Sometimes red fruits are produced. Excellent autumn colour. Prefers light shade.

Malus 'John Downie' A crab apple with white spring blossom and large gold and red fruit in autumn. Prefers full sun.

Olea europaea (olive) For a sheltered spot in full sun, the evergreen olive is superb for an internal court or basement yard. The leaves are green above and silvery-grey beneath. In a good year, it may even fruit.

Prunus incisa 'Kojo-no-mai' The name of this flowering cherry means 'dance of the butterflies', referring to the white spring flowers. There is also bronze, red and purple autumn colour and an attractive tracery of stems in winter.

Prunus x subhirtella 'Autumnalis' This cherry has delicate pink or white flowers in winter and spring and a good show of autumn colour. Prefers full sun but copes with partial shade.

Pyrus salicifolia 'Pendula' (silver pear) This tree has attractive silver foliage following spring flowers. It responds well to formative pruning and its weeping habit suits container growing. Requires full sun.

Rhus typhina 'Dissecta' (stag's horn sumach) This tree has thick, hairy new shoots and large, long, deeply cut leaves, which provide excellent autumn colour; the cones of female flowers are retained in winter. Prefers full sun but copes with partial shade.

Left: Late berries are just one of the attractions of *Clerodendron trichotomum* (glory tree).

Right: With its superb white bract 'flowers', *Cornus kousa* var. *chinensis* is perfect for the smaller courtyard.

yellow

Yellow and gold flowers and plants will look bright and cheerful whatever the time of year or the weather conditions. In a shady courtyard, they're particularly useful.

ten that demand closer inspection...

Berberis thunbergii 'Aurea' This shrub has sulphur-yellow evergreen foliage that does best in light shade.

Choisya ternata 'Sundance' (Mexican orange blossom) Butter-yellow evergreen leaves and fragrant white flowers in summer on a rounded shrub.

Crocosmia 'Citronella' Attractive, deciduous foliage is decorated with pure lemon-yellow, tubular flowers on arching stems from mid- to late summer.

Genista hispanica (Spanish gorse) This shrub has bright yellow, pea-like flowers.

Genista pilosa 'Procumbens' A low-spreading variety, ideal as ground-cover.

Forsythia x *intermedia* 'Lynwood' One of the brightest yellow forsythias. All are easy to grow and have superb yellow flowers on bare stems in early spring.

Hemerocallis 'Stella d'Oro' (daylily) This perennial has small, delicate, trumpet-shaped, golden-yellow flowers with a brown reverse. Requires full sun and moist soil.

Humulus lupulus 'Aureus' (golden hop) This can be invasive in the garden but is the perfect foliage climber for patio pots and containers.

Ilex x *altaclerensis* 'Belgica Aurea' A holly with attractive yellow-edged leaves and no spines.

Trollius europaeus (globe flower) A low-grower, flowering in late spring and early summer with golden-yellow, rounded blooms. 'Canary Bird' is one of the best.

Although a little rampant, the perennial golden hop (*Humulus lupulus* 'Aureus') will smother walls with a flush of sulphur-yellow leaves in summer.

wall

Offering a unique growing environment and the perfect support for climbers and week-stemmed shrubs, bare walls are a blessing in disguise. Even the most drab and unpromising of walls can be brightened up with a few climbers, better still some paintwork and a few climbers.

So what can you do if all you have is a wall? The quick answer is – quite a bit. Affording protection from the worst of the weather, making maximum use of the space available and creating their own individual microclimate, walls are an ideal opportunity for the no-garden gardener to do some serious planting. Some of the most interesting and exotic plants naturally climb and trail, so the choice is wide and the effects can be dramatic. The wall in question doesn't have to be anything flash. It may be the side of a house, the back of the garage, even one end of the local bus station. So long as it's sound and you have permission to put something on or against it that will not damage the mortar or rendering, it's a potential climbing frame for some really choice and showy specimens.

aesthetics

A wall in itself is rarely very interesting. It may be an attractive colour or have an attractive texture, but that's as far as it goes. Painting the wall will instantly transform it. To make it a startling feature in itself, choose a vivid colour, or pick one to link it with other elements in your home. Be a bit careful about choosing a colour: today's trendy aubergine could well be tomorrow's muddy purple. However, any error in judgement is easily and cheaply rectified so experiment a bit and see what a difference it makes. In a confined space, it's best to avoid dark colours as they can be oppressive. Paler shades will reflect light back and may well help the plants grow more strongly. Mirrors and tiles can also be used to dress up a boring wall, but remember that waterproof tile cement is essential if the effect is to be anything more than fleeting.

Those skilled with a paint brush may like to try their hand at a trompe l'oeil effect to create a mood and feeling of additional space. When done well, one of these paintings will transform the area and can look particularly convincing when mixed with the appropriate wall plants. Imagine a view over French vineyards, framed by the foliage of a grape vine and some pots of lavender at the base acting as a living foreground.

A plain red brick wall is the perfect backdrop for this very simple fountain with its eyecatching pot. The pebbles and foliage plants enhance the restful effect.

growing environment

From a horticultural perspective, the main thing to be aware of is that the direction the wall faces in will dramatically influence what will grow on or near to it. For example, a wall may be sunny or shady, or it may be a combination of both. With combination walls, those areas that get some sunshine during the day will experience much higher temperatures than those that remain in the shade.

East-facing walls get the early morning sunshine and warm up rapidly at the start of the day, while west-facing walls warm up more gradually and stay warmer for longer: well into the night, the bricks or blocks of west-facing walls act like giant night storage heaters. This means that early flowering plants on an east-facing wall may get frost damaged, and tender, later flowering exotics will be happiest on a west-facing wall.

When it comes to assessing north- and south-facing walls, it all depends on where we are gardening. Those living in the northern hemisphere will have warm, sunny, south-facing walls, while those in the southern hemisphere will have north walls that are the most favourable. In both cases, the conditions will be hotter and drier, making the site more suitable for drought-tolerant plants. The opposing walls in each instance will be cooler, moister and more shady, but with a more even temperature range.

Although our climate seems to be becoming more unpredictable, we are still at the mercy of certain winds. Walls facing the prevailing winds will be colder and harsher growing environments while those in the lee of the wind will be more sheltered and favourable.

plant maintenance

The beauty of a wall is that it will shelter the adjacent planting area, but this can be a mixed blessing. High walls and overhanging eaves will prevent natural rainfall reaching containers or planting beds at the base. Add the capillary effect, whereby porous walls can actually suck the moisture out of the soil, and we soon have some pretty inhospitable conditions to contend with.

Container plants aren't such a problem as their maintenance is very much down to us anyway: regular watering will be necessary wherever they are. Again, larger pots are easier to plant, create a greater impact and are less prone to drying out (in any case, if you chose to grow vigorous climbers and wall shrubs, they need all the root run they can get, particularly if they're going to be in that pot

which wall is which?

NORTH
(south in the southern hemisphere)
Generally cooler.
More even temperature range.
Perfect for plants that prefer a
  woodland environment.
Some plants grow less vigorously
  so may need help attaching
  themselves to the support.
Variegated plants will struggle and
  are more prone to frost damage.
Many plants recommended for
  north-facing walls may prefer the
  favourable conditions but might
  become too vigorous or invasive.

SOUTH
(north in the southern hemisphere)
Hot, especially in a good summer.
More extreme temperature
  fluctuations.
Narrow borders prone to dryness.
Perfect for some annual, half-hardy
  and tender climbers.
Perennials and shrubs can be used
  to keep the climber's roots cool.

EAST
Mild growing conditions.
Warms up quickly in the morning.
Many plants that thrive on north
  walls do well here – apart from
  some clematis and honeysuckles.
Can be problems with frost damage
  when early flower buds and new
  shoots thaw too quickly in the
  morning sun.

WEST
Mild growing conditions.
Warms up gradually during the day.
Gets the evening sun so retains heat
  into the evening and night.
One of the gentlest growing
  locations in any garden.

Above: Careful use of colour can have a dramatic effect, transforming a very dull wall into a growing focal point.

Right: Make a feature of trellis panels
and don't forget that walls are ideal for
displaying artwork.
Middle right: Tiles are ideal for adding
colour and texture.
Far right: Trompe l'oeil, or optical
illusions, can be used to add wit.

Far left: Clematis, such as *C.*'Niobe', are ideal wall plants but like a cool, moist root run and plenty of food.

Left: Ivies don't need support as they cling to walls and other plants with clinging aerial roots. A variegated cultivar, such as *H. helix* 'Goldheart', will brighten a dull corner all the year round.

Right: Wall shrubs that don't naturally cling or climb, such as this ceanothus, will need help with training wires attached to vine eyes.

of compost for many years to come). Plants in the ground will be more problematic, so it's best to plant them as far away from the base of the wall as possible. Climbers such as clematis and ivies should be planted away from the wall in soil that has been improved with plenty of organic matter, and then trained back towards the wall. This way they'll be in soil that stays moister and receives at least some of the natural rainfall available. Ground-cover plantings and generous mulches will also help, as will an automatic drip-irrigation system to mind your plants during holidays and in areas with limited access.

If you choose to grow trailing plants in hanging baskets, wall pots and windowboxes, all these will require much more maintenance than either potted plants on the ground or soil-planted plants, due to the large number of plants in a relatively small amount of soil. However, the effects can be quite stunning. Choosing a mixture of foliage, flowers and evergreens that will complement or contrast with the wall behind will provide a year-round display that will green up the barest expanse of brickwork.

support systems

Plants climb and twine in a variety of ways, and more often than not it's essential to provide them with some form of support. A few are self-clinging, usually with modified aerial roots that attach themselves to the brickwork or render. Climbing hydrangea (*Hydrangea petiolaris*) and ivy (*Hedera*) are good examples of self-clingers, and so long as the wall is sound will do no damage to the structure. However, if any maintenance needs to be done to the wall, such as painting or re-pointing, plants that twine rather than stick are a more sensible option as they can be grown on wires or trellis panels, which are easy to remove. It's imperative to keep climbing plants away from window mechanisms, heating vents, drains and gutters. Given the chance, they'll gladly climb through or along these and have the potential to cause considerable inconvenience or harm. In most cases,

it's also important to keep them away from the wall itself, mainly because good air circulation is needed to prevent any outbreaks of pests and diseases. It will also ensure that the surface of the wall doesn't become permanently damp.

Everyone's familiar with trellis, and it's the perfect way of encouraging a climbing plant to smother a particular area of wall. The trellis itself can also be given some decorative merit with a coat of paint or woodstain. Intricate designs are available, at a price, and can also be used to create the illusion of added width or depth. Clematis and jasmine, among others, will thrive on trellis, which can be lifted down from the wall should any maintenance be necessary.

For a more subtle approach, and for plants that don't naturally twine up their supports, a certain amount of training will be necessary. Roses and wall shrubs such as fremontodendron and ceanothus will need tying to their supports and here a system of vine eyes and wires will work well. Horizontal wires attached to the wall with metal vine eyes are also a good way of growing plants that have decorative trailing flowers or fruits. Wisteria blooms and bunches of grapes will be easier to enjoy as they cascade from horizontal tiers of foliage. Such plants should be tied to the supports with soft string using a figure-of-eight knot. Wire ties would soon cut into the stems, which get fatter as they grow. Make periodic checks of all ties and replace any that have become too tight.

pruning and training

Remember that training climbers horizontally will promote more side shoots which in turn will lead to more flowers and fruit. Left to rocket skywards, they'll tend to produce a good show of leaves and flowers at the top where we can't really enjoy them. It's also worth pruning climbers to keep them close to the wall. Wayward side shoots could pull the whole plant away from the wall, which isn't quite what we had in mind.

artscape

So what can you do if all you have to look out on is a plain old boring wall? Well, how about making a very simple piece of functional garden art?

This is a basic wall panel and shelf for displaying plants and sundries. The panel works as a piece of art – easily copied but very stylish; the shelf forms part of the picture. The basic principle could be scaled down or up to suit the space available and desired effect. Those with limited artistic ability needn't worry as the simplest geometric designs work best. Alternatively, copy something out of a book, or let the kids have a go.

you will need:

marine plywood
pressure-treated timber for shelf
plant pots
exterior wood paint – two colours of
    your choice and black
masking tape
jigsaw
drill and a large drill bit
paint brushes
tape measure
sandpaper
pencil and compass

REMEMBER...Secure fixing is essential, especially on walls that are subject to the prevailing winds.

1 Decide how large you want your picture to be and then measure out the marine ply and cut it to size. Remember, the larger the better.

2 Mark a line across the centre of the picture. This will be where the colours meet and where the shelf is secured. Mask the line with tape.

3 Paint one half of the ply with your first colour, taking care to cover the wood well. Apply two coats if necessary.

4 When the first colour is dry, move the masking tape over and use it to create a neat line for the second colour. Paint and allow to dry.

5 Measure the diameter of the plant pots at their halfway height and use these dimensions to mark two circles onto the shelf. Drill a pilot hole at the edge of each circle to allow the jigsaw blade access.

6 Carefully cut around the circles, making sure you keep to the line.

7 Stain or paint the shelf black and allow it to dry.

8 Use long screws to attach the shelf to the picture – drilling a pilot hole first to prevent splitting – and screwing in from the back. Paint the pots to match the shelf and fill them with plants of your choice. Use heavy-duty picture hooks to attach the picture to the wall.

This kalanchoe was chosen because it matched the picture colours perfectly. Although not hardy, the warmth of a wall and protected environment mean it would survive the summer quite happily. In the autumn it could be replaced by pots of bright red bilberries (*Vaccinium caespitosum*), bright purple winter pansies or hardy cyclamen (*Cyclamen hederifolium*). Heavy stone candle holders complete the look.

wall plant gallery

sunny walls

A sunny wall is the perfect place to grow tender and more exotic plants that will revel in the sunshine and reflected warmth of the wall.

Above: The graceful wisteria, here *W. floribunda* 'Alba', is a favourite wall plant and deservedly so with its beautiful flowers and strong constitution.

Far right: The silk tassel bush (*Garrya elliptica*) is a superb evergreen wall shrub providing interest at any time of year.

> **TIP** Choose plants carefully, especially for sunny walls. Take into account the wall colour and pick something that is going to show up well. Red-flowered climbers will get lost against a red brick wall but bright yellow or white flowers or variegated leaves would look stunning. Think before you buy, and before you plant.

ideally suited...

Actinidia kolomikta A vigorous climber with green leaves splashed with white at their tips, becoming flushed with pink as they mature. Insignificant summer flowers are fragrant.

Ceanothus (**Californian lilac**) These are superb shrubs with glorious blue flower clusters. They are lax growing but can be trained against a wall if an adequate support is available. They love full sun but not cold winds. Varieties to look out for include 'Autumnal Blue', which flowers from summer to early autumn, 'Cascade', which is a little pinker and spring flowering, and the darker 'Delight', which flowers in late spring.

Clematis 'Ernest Markham' A late-flowering variety with bright magenta flowers.

Clematis 'Niobe' Ruby-red flowers from summer into autumn. Vigorous and free-flowering.

Fremontodendron (**flannel bush**) Large yellow flowers are produced from spring through to autumn on plants with hairy evergreen leaves and stems. 'California Glory' is a deep yellow while 'Pacific Sunset' has larger, bright yellow flowers.

Jasminum officinale (**common jasmine**) Although officially deciduous, in favoured conditions, plants may hold some of their leaves during the winter. Fragrant white flowers appear in summer and autumn. The variety *affine* has flowers with a pink tinge, while 'Argenteovariegatum' has leaves with a cream margin. 'Aureum' has yellow-golden leaves.

Passiflora caerulea (**passion flower**) A climber with attractive vine-shaped leaves and complicated blue-green flowers. Look for the larger 'Grandiflora' and a pure white, scented variety 'Constance Elliott'.

Rosa 'Climbing Cécile Brünner' A rose with pale pink flowers in late summer and autumn that are complemented by deep green foliage. Vigorous. Many other roses are suitable and they are available in a wide range of colours and flower forms.

Wisteria floribunda (**Japanese wisteria**) One of the best and most beautiful climbing plants. Look out for the lilac 'Macrobotrys', the violet 'Royal Purple' and the double 'Violacea Plena'. For a pure white, try the white form of the Chinese wisteria (*Wisteria sinensis* 'Alba'). Plants need regular pruning in early spring and midsummer to keep them within bounds and may take a couple of years to start flowering. Always buy a named grafted variety as flowering can be variable with seedlings.

shady walls

Although they're lacking in natural light, shady walls can become home to many choice climbers and wall shrubs. They're particularly suitable for plants grown for autumn colour as the leaves will hold longer than if they were in a more exposed situation. Although most plants need sunshine to promote good flowering, there are also those that prefer to flower in the shade.

a good selection…

***Berberidopsis corallina* (coral plant)** A superb evergreen climber that deserves wider recognition. It bears round, red, hanging flowers in summer and early autumn.

***Clematis* 'Nelly Moser'** This pretty clematis has pinky-mauve flowers with a darker bar down the centre of each petal. Compact and free-flowering.

Clematis orientalis A vigorous and late-flowering clematis. Look out for 'Bill MacKenzie' with it's simple yellow flowers with red anthers, and fluffy winter seedheads.

Cotoneaster horizontalis A small leaved evergreen with attractive flowers and berries. Can be encouraged to clothe a wall.

***Euonymus fortunei* 'Silver Queen'** This climbing or spreading shrub has green and white-edged evergreen leaves that take on a pinkish tinge in autumn. Other excellent varieties include 'Coloratus', which turns purple in winter, and 'Emerald 'n' Gold', which has bright green leaves with yellow edges.

***Garrya elliptica* (silk tassel bush)** This has evergreen leaves and long green silky catkins in spring. A wall shrub that will need some training.

***Hedera canariensis* (Canary island ivy)** This is less hardy than *H. helix* (below), but does well on sheltered walls in towns and cities. 'Gloire de Marengo' is silvery-green with cream splashes and is also good as a houseplant.

***Hedera colchica* (Persian ivy)** Evergreen and vigorous with large leaves. 'Sulphur Heart' is splashed with gold. 'Dentata Variegata' has green leaves splashed with cream. Attractive flowerheads. Good for birds.

***Hedera helix* (English ivy)** There are many varieties of this common climber to choose from. All are evergreen and will thrive on a shady wall. Leaf shapes vary from the fine 'Maple Leaf' and 'Koniger', to the more rounded 'Perkeo'. They may be gold, as in 'Buttercup', marbled, as in 'Luzii', or variegated, as in 'Goldheart'.

***Jasminum nudiflorum* (winter jasmine)** This has fragrant, yellow flowers that appear along the stems in winter well before the leaves.

***Parthenocissus henryana* (Chinese Virginia creeper)** This is less vigorous and easier to manage than Boston ivy (below). Its deciduous leaves are an attractive green with white veins. Autumn tints.

***Parthenocissus quinquefolia* (Virginia creeper)** A vigorous self-clinging, deciduous climber with large leaves and bright red autumn tints.

***Parthenocissus tricuspidata* (Boston ivy)** This is grown for its spectacular autumn colour. Crimson and red autumn tints turn deep purple in the variety 'Veitchii'.

***Pyracantha* (firethorn)** Superb evergreen shrubs that can be grown flat against a wall on training wires or trellis panels. White spring flowers are followed by a brilliant display of autumn and winter berries. Look out for 'Mohave' with bright red berries and 'Orange Glow'. All are thorny.

***Vitis cognetiae* (vine)** Large, heart-shaped leaves turn scarlet, orange and yellow in autumn. *Vitis vinifera* 'Purpurea' is another vine, well worth growing for its attractive, deep purple leaves.

> **TIP** Plants may become spindly and drawn if they're lacking light. Pay particular attention to training, otherwise they'll grow straight up and flower well out of sight. Zigzag them across trellis panels or along horizontal training wires to keep them where they can be enjoyed. This will also encourage more side shoots and flowers.

green

Green tends to predominate in traditional gardens but in small spaces, and without the presence of a lawn, can be used as a contrast or feature colour.

top of the list...

Buxus sempervirens (box) A useful evergreen shrub for topiary, as an edging or infill plant.

Eucomis bicolor (pineapple flower) A perennial bulb with fleshy leaves on top of which is produced a green flower spike with maroon speckles. Tufts of leaves come from the top of the flower spike, hence the common name.

Euphorbia amygdaloides var. *robbiae* (Mrs Robb's bonnet) One of the finest euphorbias with evergreen leaves and lime-green 'flowers' (actually coloured bracts) in spring.

Euphorbia myrsinites This spreading evergreen plant has blue-grey stems and leaves with bright green 'flowers'.

Hebe cupressoides 'Boughton Dome' A miniature hebe forming mossy clumps of emerald-green foliage.

Hedera 'Romanze' An ivy with variegated evergreen leaves that have patches of lime-green.

Helleborus argutifolius (Corsican hellebore) This hellebore has superb evergreen foliage and pale green flowers in winter and early spring.

Nicotiana langsdorfii (tobacco plant) An annual with small, drooping, lime-green flowers in summer and early autumn.

Pelargonium tomentosum (peppermint geranium) This geranium has soft downy green leaves and white flowers in summer. Needs winter protection.

Shibataea kumasasa A dwarf bamboo with attractive green leaves and a neat habit. Perfect for containers.

Tellima grandiflora A carpeting evergreen with dainty green, bell-shaped flowers in spring.

Vinca minor (lesser periwinkle) A superb evergreen ground-cover plant with small, glossy green leaves and blue or white flowers in summer.

The base of a south-facing wall can be hot and dry and ground-cover plants need choosing carefully. This *Euphorbia myrsinites* should thrive and will appreciate the thick gravel mulch.

room

No book on gardening without a garden is complete without a look at plants actually in the home.

Although it's a totally alien environment for them, in my opinion, a room without a plant is like strawberries without cream, and there's no disputing that a few well-chosen houseplants will keep even the most frustrated green fingers happy, especially during the winter months. The plants we grow in our homes are invariably tender or tropical species that thrive in centrally heated rooms. This is a chance for us to grow weird and wonderful plants that aren't going to succumb to cold, wet winters and will probably never see a slug or a snail in their lives.

traditional & modern

Always excellent gifts – a chance to give someone a seasonal splash of colour – houseplants have been an integral part of our homes for centuries, but in recent years there's been a distinct shift towards those that flower. Supermarkets and DIY stores who adopt the 'pile them high and sell them cheap' approach to everything have been able to convince people that a plant is a disposable item. Buy it, keep it watered and enjoy the flowers, and then replace it with something else. While I wouldn't agree with this philosophy in all cases, it does make sense if space is at a premium and there are no facilities to nurture plants through their down-time when they're looking green and drab.

Plants in the home are 'designer touches' bringing the outdoors inside in lush or architectural form. Witness the popularity of sculptural cacti and succulents, which are now very much in vogue. The fact that they're easy

to look after is probably an unplanned bonus. It's the look, rather than the practicalities, that put them there in the first place. The people buying houseplants are getting younger and younger. Twenty-somethings are now as keen to furnish their homes with flora as the forty-somethings have always been. And if you look at houseplant sales throughout Europe, is it any wonder that the Scandinavians, who have the shortest gardening season, are the biggest spenders on houseplants?

the science bit

Apart from their decorative value, research is now showing that houseplants can have a positive and beneficial effect on our lives and environment. The humble spider plant (*Chlorophytum comosum* var. *variegatum*) is a good example and could be one to try if you live close to a road. In the United States, NASA scientists have discovered that this easy-to-grow houseplant can help remove up to 96 percent of the carbon monoxide found in the average room. And Dr Tove Fjeld's research at the University of Agriculture in Norway found that the presence of indoor plants can reduce feelings of fatigue, coughs, sore throats and other cold-related illnesses by more than 30 percent.

Even the strict principles of Feng Shui recognize the beneficial effects of a houseplant or two in bringing life and positive energy to a living space.

Give plants a place in your home, making them part of your decorative scheme, and they will reward you.

room by room

Continuing the theme of plants that are perfect for particular situations, here's a look at the typical home: the rooms, the conditions they provide and the plants that will love them.

living room

The living room is the most popular place for displaying indoor plants. Here they can be used to enhance existing features, such as an empty hearth, to add scale or to provide colour and decorative interest. The living room is the best place for expensive feature plants that are going to be studied and admired either individually or as a group.

growing conditions...Warm, especially in the evening. Good levels of natural light. Low humidity, particularly in winter. Most warmth in the winter when many plants should be dormant.

kitchen

The kitchen is second most popular place for houseplants, after the living room, and often doubles up as a plant 'intensive care unit'. Warmth, good natural light and the guarantee of plenty of attention mean it's the perfect place to let plants from other rooms rest or recuperate. The kitchen windowsill is the obvious site.

Other benefits of growing plants in the kitchen include the fact that the tap is handy for watering and feeding and that the extra warmth and humidity produced by washing and cooking generally favour good growth. Wall units and clear

Left: Use pots and plants to enhance your decor.
Bottom left: Matching pots and pineapple plants make a truly stylish statement.
Right: Spring flowers herald the end of winter and are always welcome.

work surfaces offer plenty of scope for interesting displays, but exterior doors can produce damaging cold draughts.

growing conditions…Warm, hot in some spots. Good light levels. High levels of humidity. Can be draughty. Plants receive plenty of attention.

hall

First impressions are important so we should make a special effort in the hallway. Unfortunately, often being narrow, dark and draughty, they tend to offer some of the least attractive growing conditions. Landings are no different, although sometimes lighter and less draughty. In the interests of safety, stairs are no place for plants, unless the treads are particularly wide and gentle. Plants must never become a hazard or interfere with the through flow of traffic.

growing conditions…Cool, especially during the day and prone to draughts. Reasonable light levels. Low levels of humidity. Confined, narrow space.

dining room

The dining room is the centre of attention at mealtimes and an area that demands special attention when entertaining. However, tables, chairs and side cabinets can mean there is little space for anything too

grand in the way of plants. Avoid flowering plants with strong scents and keep a keen eye out for insect pests.

growing conditions…Cool, especially during the day. Reasonable light levels. Low levels of humidity.

bedroom

The bedroom is very personal space where you can let your imagination run wild. Large, architectural plants will give the impression you are sleeping in a jungle.

growing conditions…Warm but usually not too warm. Reasonable natural light. Low levels of humidity. Plenty of room to grow.

bathroom

The room that's least likely to include a houseplant is the bathroom. This is strange because there are many that would relish the humid conditions. Provided there is a reasonable amount of light, many plants from warm, humid climates will thrive and help create a feeling of unashamed luxury.

growing conditions…Warm and draught free. Reasonable light levels. Medium to high humidity.

plant skates

Large houseplants add drama to the home but moving them around can be a drama in itself. Let these stylish plant skates take the strain.

Just as we like to take a breath of fresh air from time to time, so many houseplants will appreciate a spell out in the open during the summer. It's a chance for them to grow, refreshed and cleansed by summer showers and shake off the winter blues brought on by temperatures that are less than ideal, the drying effects of central heating and poor natural light. It's also the ideal opportunity to carry out some pruning, and dust can be washed away with a hose, which is quicker and more effective than those individual leaf wipes.

The opposite regime will suit many frost tender shrubs that are perfectly happy out on the patio for nine months of the year, but appreciate being moved into a porch, greenhouse or conservatory when the first frosts are forecast. Angel's trumpets (Brugmansia), oleanders (Nerium) and citrus are just three examples of large shrubs that need winter protection to survive from year to year.

the mechanics

We've agreed that we might need to move plants about, but exactly how do you drag that monster monstera out onto the balcony or haul that tree fern back into the porch? Anyone who's tried it will know that even a modest-sized plant can be almost impossible to lift. Plants have a habit of growing and what was manageable in spring can easily have become something of a problem by autumn. Plants from tropical habitats are notoriously fast-growing and have a blatant disregard for the height of ceilings or width of doors.

So, if skateboards are good enough to get our kids from A to B with a certain amount of panache, how about using them to relocate our plants? It's an idea that's been picked up by many garden centres and DIY stores but their plant skates are little more than softwood squares with a castor at each corner. Nobody has taken the trouble to develop the idea into something practical, stylish and fun. Why not make your own plant skates and turn them into works of art? Show your expertise with a paint brush and jigsaw and create something that complements the style of your home. Not only will it solve those transport problems but it can be used as a permanent display stand for plants and ornaments, as informal seating or even as a low table. And nobody will mind if you also use it to move the TV around or to help an arthritic dog to its bed. Although you could get away with just three, use at least four castors, even on the smaller skate, as it will be more stable, especially if it gets used as a seat.

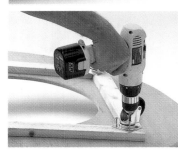

you will need:

marine plywood

wooden battens

wood glue

wood screws

spray paints suitable for wood

castors

jigsaw

drill

tape measure

pencil

string

sandpaper

1 Mark out two circles on the marine plywood, using the same point as the centre for each. Cut out carefully with a jigsaw. Drilling a pilot hole on the line of the inner circle will provide easy access for the jigsaw blade.

2 Sand both sides and the edges of the circles to produce a smooth, dust-free surface, ready for painting.

3 Cut the wooden battens to size. These are used as frames to attach the castors underneath. Turn the circles upside-down and drill pilot holes in the bottom, then

attach the battens with wood screws. A dab of glue will ensure a firm fix. Attach the castors with robust screws, using a washer if the screw head is too small.

4 Carefully spray-paint the plant skates using colours that complement each other. Several coats will give a better finish but don't spray to the point of dribbling or run-off. Plant skates that are going to be used regularly outside should be given several coats of an exterior varnish to make them completely weatherproof.

Above: Indoors or out, the plant skates will always come in handy.
Right: Choose colours to complement your decor – and maybe add your own humorous touch.

TIP When spray painting it's better to apply several thin coats rather than one thick one. It takes longer as you need to let each coat dry before applying the next, but the finish will be much smoother and more even.

room plant gallery

alight rooms

The right plant in the right room will grow happily and healthily with the minimum of care and attention.

ten easy-to-grow houseplants…

Amaryllis *(Hippeastrum hybrida)* A big bulb producing large trumpet-shaped flowers in spring.

Candle plant *(Plectranthus oertendahlii)* This low-grower has white-veined leaves with purple undersides.

Crown of thorns *(Euphorbia milii)* This spiky succulent has vivid red, tubular flowers.

Flaming Katy *(Kalanchoe blossfeldiana)* Succulent leaves and bright tubular flowers on a bushy plant.

Money plant, jade tree *(Crassula ovata)* Fleshy succulent leaves on a central trunk.

Mother-in-law's tongue *(Sanseveria trifasciata)* Tall spike-like, often

TIP If plants aren't getting enough light, they will tend to look pale and drawn and not produce the best leaf colouration.

variegated, succulent leaves.

Pineapple *(Ananas comosus* var. *variegatus)* The variegated pineapple has spiny variegated leaves and sometimes bears a brightly coloured central fruit.

Rose of China *(Hibiscus rosasinensis)* A shrubby plant with large trumpet flowers in various shades.

Spider plant *(Chlorophytum comosum* var. *variegatum)* A widely available pot plant with arching variegated leaves and trailing stems supporting baby plants.

Winter cherry *(Solanum capsicastrum)* Decorative orange, ball-shaped fruits.

CULTIVATION TIPS

Group houseplants together. More delicate plants that don't like central heating, such as ferns, will relish the moist microclimate this creates.

Left: Given plenty of light, the beautiful rose of China *(Hibiscus rosa-sinensis)* will flower for several weeks.

inside-out plants

Like us, there are some plants that are happiest outside in the summer and indoors in the winter.

houseplants that can summer outside…

Agave	Guzmania
Aeonium	Hedera
Aloe	Hypoestes
Begonia	Lampranthus
Caladium	Lantana
Calathea	Mirabilis
Chlorophytum	Monstera
Codiaeum	Platycerium
(croton)	Plectranthus
Cordyline	Sansevieria
Crassula	Solenostemon
Dracaena	Streptocarpus
Echeveria	Tillandsia
Ficus	Tradescantia
Furcraea	Vriesea
Gloriosa	

cool rooms

There are plenty of plants that can cope with a cool room, although most do prefer good light as well.

look for these beauties…

Canary date palm *(Phoenix canariensis)* This has tough palm-like leaves on large plants.

Cape leadwort *(Plumbago auriculata)* A climber with delicate blue flowers.

Dragon tree *(Dracaena marginata)* Grassy variegated leaves shoot from a central stem.

Fairy primrose *(Primula malacoides)* This has delicate leaves and fragrant flowers.

House lime *(Sparmannia africana)* A plant with large leaves and white spring flowers.

Mother-of-thousands *(Saxifraga stolonifera)* Rounded, pink-edged leaves and baby plants on hanging trails.

Partridge-breasted aloe *(Aloe variegata)* A smooth succulent with variegated leaves.

Pink jasmine *(Jasminum polyanthum)* A climber with sweetly scented flowers.

Sago palm *(Cycas revoluta)* This has stiff, arching palm-like leaves.

Silk oak *(Grevillea robusta)* Produces ferny green foliage on a large plant.

Left: Plumbago auriculata is a climber that relishes being grown in a cool environment.

warm rooms

The choice of plants is large, but they'll need more watering than those in a cooler room.

plants to make an impact...

African violet (Saintpaulia hybrids) Round hairy leaves and small violet-like flowers.

Aluminum plant (Pilea cadierei) Silvery mottled leaves.

Areca palm (Chrysalidocarpus lutescens) Typical miniature palm.

Devil's ivy (Scindapsus aureus) A climber with attractive golden-marbled leaves.

False aralia (Dizygotheca elegantissima) This has almost black, delicately fingered leaves.

Flame violet (Episcia cupreata) Attractive foliage with orange red flowers.

Flamingo flower (Anthurium andreanum) Glossy leaves and bright red tropical flowers.

Peperomia (Peperomia capreata) Fleshy leaves with pointed flower spikes.

Sweetheart plant (Philodendron scandens) Fleshy green leaves on a trailing or climbing vine.

Umbrella tree (Schefflera actinophylla) Attractive glossy green leaves.

shady rooms

Flowers are rare on houseplants that tolerate shade, but the leaves can make up for this.

shade-tolerant foliage plants...

Button fern (Pellaea rotundifolia) Tiny leaflets on wiry stems.

Cast iron plant (Aspidistra elatior) Leathery dark green leaves.

Chinese evergreen (Aglaonema commutatum) An attractive foliage plant, sometimes with interesting markings.

Hare's foot fern (Davallia canariensis) A delicate fern that creeps via hairy rhizomes.

Holly fern (Cyrtomium falcatum) An unusual fern that copes well with draughts.

Ivy tree (Fatshedera lizei) Thick ivy-like leaves are produced on a central trunk.

Painted net leaf (Fittonia verschaffeltii) A small, spreading plant with a pale intricate pattern on the leaves.

Rex begonia (Begonia rex) Showy leaves in a variety of colours.

Staghorn fern (Platycerium bifurcatum) Large thick green fronds.

Umbrella plant (Cyperus alternifolius) This plant has grassy leaves radiating from the top of tall stems.

Left: Aluminium plant (Pilea cadierei) has silver-marked leaves.
Above centre: Arum or calla lily (Zantedeschia aethiopica).
Above right: Mixed display of cacti and succulents.

plants we can't kill

Even houseplants follow the seasons, usually influenced by the available light, and have a growing season and a dormant season. More houseplants die through being overwatered than for any other reason.

plants that can be overwatered...

Arum or calla lily (Zantedeschia aethiopica) Attractive dark green foliage and large white spathes (bracts surrounding the spikes of flowers). Look out for pink Z. rehmannii and yellow Z. elliottiana and the many and varied hybrids.

Azaleas These really hate drying out, especially in the winter when they're in flower. Dilute liquid feeds will also encourage prolonged flowering.

Ferns Ferns don't like being waterlogged but do like a moist atmosphere, so regular misting will pay dividends. Grouping a few together will also create a moist microclimate.

Umbrella plant (Cyperus alternifolius) This is a waterside plant with slender stems and grassy leaves radiating from the tip, just like the spokes of an umbrella. Look out for the variegated form 'Variegatus' and the smaller 'Gracilis'.

plants we can occasionally forget to water...

Cacti and succulents These come in a range of shapes and sizes and are always unusual and trendy, ideal for creating a contemporary look. They're used to storing water so can cope really well.

Pelargoniums Often erroneously referred to as geraniums, they have big, blowsy flowers and often colourful leaves. Some have scented foliage and all will cope with dry conditions.

Bromeliads These, which include Guzmania, Nidularium and Aechmea, have stiff, often spotted or striped leaves and sometimes bright, long-lasting flower spikes. The leaves form a rosette with a central 'urn' that should be kept topped up with water, but it doesn't need doing very often.

blue

Blue is important as a contrast colour, and it can be used to cool down a planting scheme. Fairly trendy now, there was a time when blue flowers were much more difficult to find.

eight that are worth a try...

Campanula isophylla (Italian bellflower) This is hard to beat for the number of pale blue flowers it produces on its trailing stems.

Ceanothus 'Blue Mound' (Californian lilac) One of the best and less vigorous of the Californian lilacs, this forms mounds of dark blue flowers. It is ideal for cascading out of a large planter or through the railings of a balcony.

Ceratostigma willmottianum Green leaves with pink tips set off the attractive blue flowers. A good all-round performer.

Clematis alpina Flowering from spring through to early summer, this daintly clematis has beautiful blue flowers with white centres. Fluffy seedheads continue the interest into autumn.

Echinops ritro (globe thistle) Bright blue globes of flower are borne above attractive spiky leaves. Prefers full sun and poor soil but will tolerate shade.

Eryngium alpinum 'Blue Star' (sea holly) Vivid blue thistle-like flowers have attractive bracts at the base. Deep rooting so needs open soil or a deep pot to be happy.

Festuca glauca (blue fescue) This is a clump-forming evergreen grass with vivid silvery-blue leaves. Fine in hot, dry conditions.

Meconopsis betonicifolia (Himalayan blue poppy) This lovely poppy likes cool, damp summers so would be ideal for courtyards or balconies that are sheltered from the sun and wind. It dies after flowering.

> **TIP** As a contrast colour, blue works particularly well with orange and yellow.

The globe thistle, *Echinops ritro*

balcony

Extend your home onto your balcony, grow interesting plants and make the most of the view.

The chances are that if there is a balcony in your home, it's been put there for a reason. It may be designed to provide valuable additional living space and allow access outside for a breath of fresh air. It may also be a vantage point from which to admire a spectacular view. Yet, when you walk around any major town or city, it's disappointing to see how many balconies are left dull and lifeless as their owners fail to see their potential as a space for gardening. We've paid for this facility so why not make the most of it?

For the would-be gardener a balcony is something of a challenge. Like a patio or terrace, once the green fingers start twitching, it will always end up being too small. And in the process, it's all too easy for it to become so crowded with plants that there's no room left for sitting or entertaining. The trick is to achieve a balance between horticultural enthusiasm and practicality. The first consideration should be what role the balcony has to play. If it's for relaxation and entertaining then space must be left for tables, chairs and possibly a lounger. If it is to be purely for plants then by all means fill it to the brim with containers, but bear in mind that they'll all need looking after. A careful combination of the two very often offers the best of both worlds.

rules and regulations

Before you start making plans, check you're not going to break the law. Flats are subject to strict building regulations when it comes to changing anything to do with their outside appearance. As part of a block, the balcony usually has to be in keeping with the rest. This means it may not be possible to erect glass screens, trellis panels or even paint the existing railings a different colour. It's worthwhile checking out these regulations beforehand, either in your title deeds, with the freeholder or under the tenancy agreement.

don't overload

And whatever you do, don't overload your balcony. It's probably been designed to take the weight of a good number of people, but large pots of compost, stone ornaments and that small water feature can weigh pretty heavily on the support beams, and the minds of the people below.

If you have extravagant plans or they involve large compost-filled planters, then it's wise to seek the advice of a structural engineer. Remember, too, that access to the balcony is limited. Not only will all the plants, compost, statues and sundries have to fit in the lift or be carried up the stairs, they'll also have to come through the flat and over that expensive new carpet.

With careful planning and considered planting, the balcony can become a virtual garden in the sky.

growing environment

Gardening on a balcony will always involve a series of compromises. Spectacular views must be kept clear, but shelter may be needed from strong winds and prying eyes. Light levels may also change dramatically from the balcony's outside edge to the side of the building. Depending on the aspect, some balconies will be warm and sunny while others are cool and shady. Temperature fluctuations can be extreme, altering massively in a matter of minutes. However, adjacent walls may offer protection to plants, with radiated heat keeping them warmer in winter, or shade keeping them cool and moist in summer. Many influences come into play, some beneficial, others down right difficult.

the wind factor

Some balconies will receive the full force of the prevailing wind, while others will be sheltered from all but the worst winter storm. Nearby buildings will also have an effect, channelling the slightest breeze into something more forceful as it squeezes between and around anything in its path.

To be able to enjoy any balcony, shelter from strong winds is essential. There's no point having a beautiful collection of plants or a fantastic view, if you can't sit out and enjoy them. Plants, too, will suffer as the wind draws moisture from the leaves, resulting in plant stress, scorching and physical damage. Some form of screening is essential, designed to diffuse the wind but still allow through plenty of light and let us make the most of the view beyond.

There are basically two options: create something artificial, perhaps with glass, metal, wood, trellis or fabric, or grow some tough evergreen shrubs and climbers that will tolerate the conditions and shelter more tender plants, and us, from the elements.

Glass is the best option, if you have the budget and can find someone who specializes in such work. Erected as a windbreak, it will quickly turn an exposed, unusable area into a sheltered enclave. It should be toughened and thick enough to withstand the elements and the occasional knock, but preferably clear, so light will still get into the adjacent rooms and the views will be maintained. Specialist glaziers will be able to offer individual advice according to the situation and existing balustrade or railings.

Trellis, willow panels, rush or bamboo screens are also effective and can be installed by anyone competent at basic DIY. They also cost a good deal less than glass. The fact that they'll filter the wind, rather than deflect it up over the top, means that plants on the sheltered side will not get buffeted from above. Such screens will knock out some light, and part of the view, but when erected on the

> **REMEMBER...** Everything on the balcony must be securely anchored, perhaps with a length of wire attached to a robust hook on the wall behind. Wall pots must be firmly fixed, so they can't plunge to the street below. Even large plants in heavy containers can easily be dislodged by gusts of wind. Any large shrub, particularly if it's evergreen, will need quite a bit of care. In a restricted amount of compost, plants will only stay happy and healthy if they are fed and watered regularly, particularly during warm or windy spells of weather.

Left: The aspect and climate make a big difference to what you can grow on the balcony. In a warm climate you can even try your hand at a grape vine

Right: Even the narrowest balcony can become a garden space to share.

side of the prevailing winds, they'll make the rest of the space more useable. What's more, their open structure makes them ideal for a wide range of annual and perennial climbing plants. In a few months they can be clothed in growth, making good use of the space and contributing a fine show of flower and foliage colour.

If there's room for some reasonable-sized planters then a growing screen or hedge could be an option. This too will filter the wind and again contributes to the style of the balcony. It will also catch and deflect any rain. Plants can be clipped into cones, columns, balls or fanciful shapes so they become features in themselves, adding structure and colour right through the year. What could be nicer than sitting in the warm on a winter's day with a couple of bright green peacocks for company? However, don't plant too enthusiastically, or very soon too much light will be blocked out from the flat itself. A filtering foliage screen is the answer, like living net curtains, so we can see out but nobody can see in.

vistas & eyesores

The next task is to decide what we want to keep on the balcony and what needs altering. Views may be good or bad: some people are lucky and have adjacent parks, squares or rivers to enjoy, others may have a panoramic view of the gas works, railway station or motorway – just as interesting, but not all that enchanting.

Balconies that overlook anything less than spectacular could do with the judicious placement of a screen or plant that will disguise the offending item. It's surprising what one potted evergreen shrub will do in the way of blotting out an eyesore, no matter how large it is. Because it's closer to the eye, the plant can obliterate the view of a large building or electricity pylon quite effectively.

Where a balcony faces another building, a bit of screening may be necessary in the interests of modesty and decency. There's something strangely addictive about looking through other people's windows, especially when it's dark and the people inside shine out like beacons. If you suspect that your neighbours are looking at you, then adding a few plants to divert their gaze can be a wise precaution.

design ideas

I've always been a bit sceptical about the saying 'less is more', but with garden design I think it often holds true. A simple layout with a few stunning features often works far better than the most intricate of designs. In a limited space, such as a balcony (or roof) garden, it's well worth limiting our inclination to fill every corner and cover every surface. One spectacular planter can have far more impact and is much easier to look after than a motley collection of pots and planters scattered all over the place. Flooring, wall paints, pots and lights can be chosen to link with the colours or materials used in the adjacent room. The effect will be one of a more cohesive design, extending the room out onto the balcony and making the planting a much more integral part of the home.

First, assess the space. Look for the positive points, as well as the potential problems.

floor

Most balconies are surfaced with concrete or bitumen, which may be fine as a base. They're both hard wearing and will cope well with being damp. However, in such a small area, that's very much part of the adjacent room, it's a good idea to pay particular attention to the flooring. With perhaps just a few square metres to deal with, a change will not cost a fortune and could form the basis to a much more attractive display.

Ceramic tiles or decking are a practical and aesthetically pleasing solution, and can be laid with the minimum of disruption. Make sure the tiles are frost proof and non-slip. Decking is warm underfoot, allows free drainage and can be stained or painted to match the existing decor. It will also spread the weight evenly over the entire surface area.

It's a good idea to think of the balcony as a room, after all it has walls, a floor and sometimes even a ceiling. Pay particular attention to the materials used and the colours and textures they provide. Even the most spectacular plants will not disguise a floor that should have been repaired, or walls in desperate need of a lick of paint.

walls

With any balcony there are plenty of walls to play with. Using all the available space means that trellis panels, wall pots, mirrors or wall fountains can all be incorporated, without sacrificing ground space. Making the most of this 'third dimension' is the secret to creating an attractive balcony garden without rendering the balcony itself unusable.

Although there may be regulations governing our choices, the colour of the walls should be considered. If there is the opportunity to make a change, think carefully before splashing out with the latest designer colour. Subtle, muted colour schemes are better for showing off plants. Bright, trendy colours and paint effects date quickly and can be overpowering. It's much better to let the plants and flowers add the colour and change them as the seasons or changing fashions dictate.

Wall pots are perfect for the balcony and available in a multitude of materials, styles and colours. However, they can only contain a small volume of compost and, on a warm wall, they will be prone to drying out on hot summer days.

balustrades

Balustrades are very often rather basic in design. However, they do provide an excellent framework up which to grow climbing and trailing plants, while still allowing sight of the view beyond. A few climbing annuals in a low trough or planter will soon clothe them in foliage and flower. You might also like to consider adding your own customizing touches, perhaps a smart wooden hand rail or ropes and twines woven into attractive patterns between the rails.

nitty gritty

On a practical note, we should consider storage and lighting. Balconies very often become a dumping ground for all sorts of household detritus. A good-sized storage cupboard will keep all life's essentials out of sight. The lack of a shed, attic or garage doesn't have to mean that we have to spend our time looking out onto a balcony that's proudly sporting an old bicycle and the stepladder. Look for stacking or folding tables and chairs that can be stored away in winter, or choose furniture that can be used inside and out – perhaps on the balcony and in the kitchen. Hammocks are great – if a little difficult to get out of – and with sturdy walls at our disposal, they're a space-effective option. They can be stored away easily – unlike a traditional lounger. When choosing a site to hang it, just make sure that the hammock can't empty you out over the railings when you use it.

Lights are also worth considering, both from a functional point of view and for the decorative effects that they can create. A balcony that has been lit to highlight, floodlight or downlight specimen plants and interesting features will look as good from inside looking out as it does outside. Lights also mean you can garden at night and easily see what you are doing. And you can also use candles to create a special ambience and allow guests to take in the view, and plantings, without being dazzled.

Right: Making use of natural features, such as this tree, can influence the design of a balcony area with dramatic results.

planting the balcony

Large planters are the order of the day. With fewer to look after and a greater volume of compost in each, they're easier to plant and simpler to maintain. Place them in their final positions before reaching for the compost. Make sure they won't be in the way. Corners are an obvious place. Remember to keep access doors and windows free for safety's sake.

Plant in sympathy with the elements, and life will be much easier; ignore them, and you'll have one long round of disappointments. It's vital to assess the conditions your balcony provides, and plan and plant accordingly. Shrubs are a good starting point as they provide a permanent structure and framework for more transient plants, like bulbs and seasonal bedding. As they're going to be in their pots for several years, make sure they're planted well, in good quality compost. Make the most of the few plants you have by choosing those with several seasons of interest. Think, too, about growing one plant through another so they compensate for each other's shortcomings, and provide the best show in the space available.

Don't think that once planted things can't be changed. Even the most experienced gardeners are constantly moving plants and changing their ideas. Don't be afraid to experiment, buying something new each year and discarding plants that seem to malinger in their pots. Be prepared to accept when a colour combination doesn't work, or something simply refuses to grow, and get rid of it. In a small space, the plants have to perform – and perform well – otherwise they're not worth the area they're occupying. Similarly, as the seasons change, and plants perform at different times of the year, move plants that are reaching their peak into more prominent positions so they can be enjoyed to the full. Those that have finished flowering or have yet to put on a show can be shunted to the back, or used as foliage fillers to balance a display.

Try to include a number of scented plants, particularly those that release their perfume at night. The close confines of a balcony will mean that these scents are magnified, particularly on warm, still summer evenings. With a balcony, we have the luxury of being able to leave doors and windows open at night to continue enjoying these fragrances, something our terrestrial gardening neighbours can't do for fear of being burgled.

With just a limited space, and a restricted number of plants to buy, think about developing a theme to the planting, perhaps a particular

TIPS

- Larger containers have more impact and are easier to look after.
- Plants tend to grow towards the light so need turning regularly.
- Use loamless compost as it's lighter and cleaner to handle.
- Anchor plants that could be caught by the wind and blown over the edge.
- Inspect plants regularly and trim off excessive growth.
- Water with care, and regularly, but avoiding too much run off.
- Move plants around to create an ever-changing display.

colour or a collection from one family of plants. Being able to grow a range of closely related plants gives a fascinating insight into the intricacies and diversity to be found in nature.

watering

Watering can be a problem, and the question of drainage should be considered well before planting begins. Any water applied to balcony plants will need somewhere to go – preferably not straight down onto the neighbours below.

Of course the balcony itself will have been designed to cope with a certain about of run-off water, but not the quantities that a lush planting of shrubs, perennials and seasonal bedding plants will require. Minimize the problems by limiting watering only when necessary and using saucers and water-absorbing gels. Or consider installing an automated drip irrigation system to enable the plants to look after themselves. However, remember those drying winds – it's still important to check your plants regularly.

special features

Just because we're dealing with a small space, doesn't mean we can't include a feature or two. Every garden needs a focal point and a balcony is no exception, no matter how stunning the view may be. At night the balcony itself will become the view, and as such should be interesting to look at.

water

It may sound ridiculous, but it's perfectly possible to have a stunning water feature, even on the smallest balcony. In a city centre, the gentle sound of running water is a perfect way of diverting attention from traffic noise that permeates up to the balcony from the street below.

On any balcony, the walls can be used in a variety of ways. One of the best is to incorporate a wall fountain. With such a range of realistically priced low-voltage pond pumps available, installing a fountain is a simple task, even for the less experienced. Small plastic water tanks can easily be transformed into miniature pools, offering room enough for a small lily, a marginal or two and a handful of floating plants. Add a fish or two, and we've all the joys of a full-sized pond, without any of the hassle. The water level may need topping up from time to time, but that's a small price to pay for the opportunity to grow such a rich and varied range of water plants.

Any feature that includes moving water will require an electricity supply. There are solar powered pond pumps available but until sunshine can be guaranteed just when you want it, a mains supply and low voltage transformer are the more reliable option. All electrical garden products come with clear and accurate manufacturer's instructions but if you are in any doubt about installing your own pump or garden lighting, always consult a qualified electrician. It's a wise precaution and will be money well spent.

wildlife gardening

Assuming you don't have a cat in the flat, balconies can become wildlife havens. Inner city areas are devoid of many of the plants and habitats that these creatures need to survive. Although small water features are unlikely to attract the usual contingent of frogs and toads, they will get the attention of dragon and damselflies, keen to lay their eggs, in summer. They will also become a watering hole for many insects and birds. Berried plants can be planted to encourage wild birds in the winter, and a bird table and bird bath will become a lifeline during cold, harsh spells.

Come the spring and many balcony gardeners will find they are sharing their potted shrubs and wall plants with nesting birds. Passing butterflies and bees will also happily pollinate any fruit and vegetables we choose to grow. The garden in the sky can be a really valuable addition to the natural flora and fauna of the neighbourhood.

Left: Balcony supports can easily be turned into an excellent natural growing habitat for plants.

Right: Use one wall for a stunning focal point, such as this eccentric water fountain.

screen two

Gardening on a balcony needs careful thought. It's good to do something that's imaginative but it also has to be practical.

Being high up, a balcony is going to be prone to the vagaries of the weather, and wind will feature on the agenda quite frequently – strong at times and gale-force occasionally. Even the slightest breeze can topple a large plant so anything growing on a balcony needs to be fairly sturdy and preferably anchored to an adjacent wall or railing.

Trellis screens are ideal for balconies as they provide a perfect support for climbing and trailing plants and make the most of the small amount of space that's available. They'll also look great from indoors but still allow light into the adjacent rooms and views though to those far-reaching vistas.

Anyone who's put up a wooden panel fence in a windy spot will know that even moderate winds can be disastrous. This is because the fence presents an impenetrable barrier and is hit by the full force of the wind, which then swirls up over the top and down the other side,

so even plants on the leeward side can be flattened. Hedges and trellis in a similar spot have quite the opposite effect. Allowing some air to pass through, they effectively filter the wind, reducing its strength and slowing it down. So trellis is an ideal choice for use on a balcony.

The vast majority of architects don't live in the buildings they design, which is probably why the balconies of flats invariably sit side-by-side. This is great if you get on with your neighbours and they're as keen to keep things looking as good as you are. Sadly, this isn't always the case, so a trellis screen can be vital to provide you with some much needed privacy. And where a balcony is overlooked, again a section of trellis will form an attractive and functional screen.

This easy to construct yet very effective screen has a framework of bold black lines, filled in with soft colours, making the most of interesting and muted shades of stained glass. The basic construction principles could be applied to a variety of materials and locations – or you could customize a ready-made piece of trellis. Just make sure it's strong and firmly attached to the railings or walls of your balcony before you plant. Capitalize on the fact that light will come through the trellis and experiment with clear and opaque coloured glass or Perspex.

Left: It's possible to grow flowers, fruit and vegetables on a balcony. Here are alpine strawberries, pansies in a wide variety of colours and a selection of foliage plants.

Far right (top): Here a yellow pansy has been chosen to complement the yellow glass and black framework. Summer bedding plants are great for small containers as they can cope with the extreme conditions – and always seem to be in flower.

TIP Trellis can be quickly and easily removed for maintenance of railings and walls, and there is the option of taking the whole thing with you if and when you move.

you will need:

pressure-treated wood

coloured glass or Perspex

exterior woodstain or spray paint

wood glue

exterior adhesive

screws

containers – loaf tins are ideal

galvanized wire

saw

drill

tape measure

1 Measure up the section of balcony you wish to decorate and construct a trellis frame to fit. Try to use pressure-treated timber as it will last a lot longer. Glue and screw the pieces together for greater strength.

2 Spray the frame the colour of your choice. Black is a good option, making the finished screen recreate the look of a stained glass window.

3 Cut sections of Perspex to fit a few of the gaps in the trellis, or get your local glazier to cut pieces of coloured glass to fit, and fix them in place with exterior adhesive. Don't be tempted to fill too many of the gaps. Aim for a balance between light and colour and the view beyond.

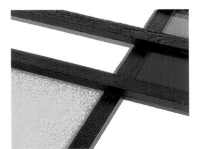

4 Leave the adhesive to set before moving on to the next stage. The glass or Perspex can be held in position with tape until the adhesive has thoroughly set.

5 Spray the planters so they're the same colour as the trellis frame. These metals tins are ideal – strong, lightweight and cheap. They're also easy to fix to the trellis with lengths of galvanized wire. Whatever container you use, make sure it has plenty of draining holes. Fill with good quality potting compost and you're ready to plant.

balcony plant gallery

living screens

On a balcony or roof it may be necessary to create some privacy or provide protection from prevailing winds. Instead of trellis or fence panels, try growing a living screen that will also add colour and interest in such a limited space. Being evergreen they'll need looking after all year round, but the effect is worth the effort.

a dozen plants to try…

Buxus sempervirens (common box) A plant with a multitude of uses: it's superb as a small evergreen screen. It has small leaves that can be trimmed with shears, without leaving unsightly cuts.

Carpinus betulus (hornbeam) This tree is similar to beech (below) but with longer, thinner, toothed leaves. The variety 'Columnaris' is slow-growing and very dense so forms an effective screen that will not need quite as much pruning.

Elaeagnus x ebbingei A hard-working evergreen shrub with attractive leaves and a tough constitution.

Fagus sylvatica (beech) A very traditional deciduous hedging plant. Clipping seems to encourage the plants to hang on to some of the dead leaves.

Genista aetnensis (Mount Etna broom) For something a little different try this fine evergreen with its whippy stems and attractive yellow flowers. It copes well with strong winds.

Ilex aquifolium (holly) This is a really tough plant that responds well to regular pruning. The prickly leaves could be a problem in a very confined space but with the attraction of winter berries who could resist it?

Ligustrum ovalifolium (privet) Another traditional evergreen hedging plant, well suited to gardens in small spaces. The golden-leaved 'Aureum' is superb while the leaves of 'Argenteum' are edged with white.

Lonicera nitida A very dense evergreen shrub with small, rounded leaves. Scented spring flowers and purple autumn berries add interest. Look for the golden-leaved 'Baggesen's Gold' to brighten up a shady corner.

Phyllostachys (bamboo) Look out for *Phyllostachys aurea* and *P. aureosulcata*, which form good screens and are happy growing in containers. Bamboos can be vigorous but some are ideal for a more contemporary setting.

Pinus mugo (dwarf mountain pine) This is one of several pines that are perfect for an oriental themed roof or balcony.

Tamarix ramosissima (tamarisk) A light, feathery shrub with attractive leaves and plumes of white or pink flowers in late summer. It should be pruned hard, almost to the ground, after planting to encourage a strong, stable root system.

Taxus baccata (yew) A deep green conifer that is surprisingly fast-growing. Remember the bright red berries are poisonous to humans (although birds will love them). Look out for the golden forms 'Fastigiata Aurea' and 'Standishii'.

> **TIP** Trim large leaved evergreens with secateurs, rather than shears, to avoid cutting through too many of the leaves. It will take longer but produces a much neater finish and plants will stand close scrutiny.

Left: Dwarf pines, such as *Pinus mugo* 'Winter Gold', are superb specimen plants for pots.
Right: Pretty flowers, lush leaves and berries for the birds, what more could you want from the Himalayan honeysuckle (*Leycesteria formosa*)?

plants for wildlife

In towns and cities we should be prepared to share our garden spaces with local wildlife.

plants that help…

Lavandula angustifolia (lavender) Evergreen scented foliage, summer flowers and attractive to bees and butterflies.

Leycesteria formosa (Himalayan honeysuckle) This shrub produces pendent white flowers surrounded by red bracts in summer, followed by purple berries in autumn. Birds love them.

Mahonia aquifolium (Oregon grape) Superb evergreen with scented spring flowers for us, and berries for the birds.

Limnanthes douglasii (poached egg plant) An annual with ferny foliage smothered in yellow-centred, white flowers in summer and autumn. Attracts bees and hoverflies.

Salvia officinalis (common sage) Evergreen spreading plant with purple summer flowers that are attractive to butterflies.

aquatics

Gardenless living doesn't preclude a water feature and the chance to grow some interesting aquatic plants. For small containers, choose just one or two plants so the water doesn't get overcrowded.

some for flowers...

Caltha palustris (marsh marigold) Beautiful early spring marigold flowers. The white form 'Plena' is smaller and so suitable for very small water features.

Iris pseudacorus 'Variegata' (variegated flag iris) This produces the typical yellow iris flowers and yellow and green striped leaves.

Mentha aquatica (water mint) With its distinctive mint smell and purple flowers, this is best in a small contained water feature as it's too invasive for ponds.

Mimulus guttatus (monkey musk) A most rewarding marginal plant with colourful, sometimes spotted, snapdragon-shaped flowers. Flowers are produced from spring through to autumn.

some for foliage...

Carex elata 'Aurea' (Bowles' golden sedge) Fabulous golden leaves with a graceful arching habit and seedheads in late summer.

Houttuynia cordata 'Chameleon' (houttuynia) Spade-shaped leaves splashed with green, cream and red. Small white flowers. Very vigorous.

Scirpus zebrinus (zebra rush) Leaves horizontally striped with green and white.

Typha minima (dwarf reed mace) This produces flowerheads like miniature bulrushes and is perfect for the smallest water feature.

Below: The marsh marigold (*Caltha palustris*) is one aquatic that will thrive in a small pond and flower in early spring.

alpines

Inhospitable conditions are often enjoyed by plants from more extreme parts of the world. Those from alpine regions can cope well with cold, windswept roofs and balconies and relatively poor soil. All they ask is a free-draining compost and protection from the worst of the winter rains. Try growing a collection in a half pot, shallow dish or windowbox. They're small but beautiful and worth putting somewhere where they'll be enjoyed at close quarters.

five to grow are...

Armeria maritima (thrift) This forms neat evergreen cushions of foliage and round, pompon flowerheads.

Dianthus alpinus (pink) A miniature pink, producing cushions of foliage and delicate, scented flowers in late spring.

Gentiana sino-ornata (gentian) An autumn-flowering, semi-evergreen, spreading perennial with large blue trumpet flowers.

Lewisia cotyledon This little plant produces fleshy leaved rosettes with brightly coloured flowers in early summer.

Saxifraga 'Tumbling Waters' A spring-flowering, evergreen, carpeting plant with flower sprays covered in hundreds of miniature white blooms.

also worth trying are...

Androsace carnea
Arenaria balearica
Draba aizoides
Gentiana saxosa
Gentiana verna
Primula pubescens
Sedum spathulifolium
Sempervivum

A collection of miniature alpines looks great in pots and is a good way of extending the range of plants that can be grown. *Dianthus alpinus* is a good one to start with.

TIP Dress the compost of alpines with decorative aggregate mulches to keep the neck of the plants dry and prevent flowers and foliage getting splashed with wet compost.

mauve

Somewhere between red and blue, mauve plants are best contrasted with orange or yellow for a dramatic effect. It's a warm colour but can get lost in an overly colourful planting scheme.

my favourites include…

Erysimum 'Bowles Mauve' **(perennial wallflower)** A mass of mauve flowers from winter to midsummer.

Gaultheria mucronata 'Mulberry Wine' A superb evergreen with bright red-purple autumn berries. Prefers shade.

Helleborus hybridus 'Pluto' An unusual hellebore with deep purple flowers that are shaded green-purple inside.

Hemerocallis 'Grape Velvet' A hardy daylily bearing wine-purple flowers with a green throat in summer. Likes full sun.

Liriope muscari A small evergreen plant with strappy leaves and mauve autumn flower spikes.

Prunella grandiflora **(self heal)** A low, spreading, semi-evergreen with attractive spikes of purple flowers in summer.

Polemonium reptans **(Jacob's ladder)** Small, lilac flowers in summer on low, mound-forming plants. The pretty leaves are composed of many small leaflets.

Rhodochiton atrosanguineus **(purple bell vine)** An unusual climber for a warm wall, with mauve and purple bell-shaped flowers produced in summer and early autumn. Needs winter protection.

Solanum crispum 'Glasnevin' **(potato vine)** A vigorous evergreen climber bearing attractive purple summer flowers with bright yellow centres.

Verbena bonariensis A frost hardy perennial with stiff, upright stems bearing small heads of lilac-purple flowers from midsummer to early autumn.

Viola labradorica 'Purpurea' A purple-leaved violet that flowers from early spring right through to summer. Perfect for a small pot or as an underplanting.

With their built-in yellow contrasting centres, the mauve flowers of *Solanum crispum* 'Glasnevin' really take some beating.

roof

High up above the roof tops, you can create a private space that makes the most of the surrounding views and sunshine.

As towns and cities become more congested, planners and developers are forever reaching skywards. City living spaces are an exciting alternative for the reluctant commuter, and for the gardener, they present something of a challenge. Quite apart from the mild attack of vertigo they may trigger, roof gardens usually mean that everything has to be carted up several flights of stairs and the plantings will have to endure some pretty extreme conditions.

With a little foresight, and a keen eye for design, it's possible to create a rooftop garden in the smallest of spaces that, weather permitting, will also add to that over-stretched living space. It can become the perfect place to relax in the evening, well above the hustle and bustle beneath and away from prying eyes. And there's no denying that that extra space, providing it is

carefully planned and planted, will add value to the property even to a non-gardening prospective purchaser. At a time when every trick in the book is being used to enhance properties, the horticultural tack is seen as cost-effective and attractive. Good gardens sell houses, and roof gardens that are practical and useable help sell flats.

However, first let's look at the practicality of developing a roof garden. It's probably all going to sound very depressing, but roofs are awkward things and need to be treated with care – you don't want to be faced with thousands in court costs, building fees and the wrath of disgruntled neighbours. Those living in flats where the prospect of roof-top development is a viable proposition will already be wise to the fact, and the following should provide some useful and practical pointers for the rest.

Built-in storage, such as this aluminium and wood seating, doesn't have to be obtrusive. Canopies can be used for shade, shelter and privacy. They can also add a strong architectural element.

assess the site

Many frustrated gardeners dream of having a roof garden, but for a variety of reasons, not all roofs are suitable. The first, and most obvious, is the fact that most are pitched. Add the fact that they're also usually tiled, and the whole concept of getting plants to grow up there and maintain them is a non-starter.

safety

Safety should be of paramount importance: the safety of whoever will use or maintain the garden, the safety of those below and on the surrounding streets and the safety of any people living in the rest of the building who also rely on your roof. Ignore any of these points and you're courting disaster.

First, if the roof area is adjacent to your flat, what about the people underneath it? The roof is probably more valuable to them and may well be wrapped up in their title deeds. Check that you have permission to develop the area. You may even have to apply for permission to change its use.

Second, any roof space that's to be used as a garden must be strong enough and durable enough to put up with the extra moisture and wear and tear that this will inevitably involve. You must call in a qualified surveyor or structural engineer to assess any physical limitations. Although they'll charge for a survey, it will be a good deal cheaper than having to repair any damage done – however innocently. A roof space is governed by the same set of structural considerations as those that apply to a balcony. Are the support beams strong enough? Will the surfacing stay waterproof under planters of heavy compost? Is there a safety rail or balustrade? Is there adequate drainage for excess water? If you've any doubt about any of these points, it's best to leave well alone, or set about doing some building work to ensure that your proposed garden meets with any planning and building regulations that may apply.

practicality

The second set of considerations relates to whether developing the roof area is a practical proposition. Even with a flat roof there are considerable limitations. The roof surface itself is the most obvious. Unfortunately most are covered in bitumen felt because it's an effective, quick and comparatively cheap option for the builders. But, it's not designed for walking on, particularly as the stone chippings, added for durability, will quickly perforate the felt beneath. Any maintenance of a garden on bitumen felt will need to

be done from boards to spread the weight evenly over the surface. To develop such areas, we really need to consider changing the surface or at least covering it with decking.

The roof may be able to cope with anything you want to do, but then there's the question of access. Is it possible to get pots, compost, plants, paving or decking materials up there in the first place? Buildings with lifts are fine unless you want to transport anything that's abnormally long. And, once the garden is made, is it easy to get out there to water the plants and enjoy what you've created? It may be that there's no door to the area and access is via a window. Remember that anything that's in the least bit awkward at first will become more so as time goes by. And just how are you going to get rid of old compost, clippings and all the debris a garden can generate over a period of twelve months?

One thing every roof gardener should do is keep everything as light as possible. It will reduce the stresses and strains on the roof itself, and on the gardener who has to get the materials up there in the first place. Simple ideas such as using plastic pots instead of terracotta, wood for raised planters instead of brick, and decking instead of traditional paving, will all help. Lightweight peat-based compost is also essential.

what's already there?

Top of the list should be adequate drainage. Roofs are designed to collect water and channel it to where it's supposed to go. Interrupt this state of affairs and you or your neighbours will soon know about it. So anything you add or take away should not hinder the progress of rainwater (or added water) towards drainage gullies and gutters.

Next, your roof might possess an interesting array of obstacles. Those essentials of modern day life – a healthy crop of aerials, vents and cables – all have to be worked around. Chimneys need special attention as they're designed to take away potentially harmful gases and may well prevent use of the area. Satellite dishes, TV aerials, skylights and cables are easier to cope with – to disguise or make a feature of, whichever you prefer.

The simplest designs always make the best use of available space so don't go overboard with beds and planters, changes of level or materials. We're supposed to be creating additional living space rather than clutter.

growing environment

Having dealt with the logistics, the pitfalls and the possibilities, it's wise to consider the area from a plant's perspective. There's no point having a superb roof space if nothing will grow there.

One thing we can bank on is having plenty of sunshine. In addition, roofs will be subject to extreme temperature fluctuations, bereft of shelter from adjacent walls and rarely have any natural shade. Most roof spaces are exposed to the elements at all times. They'll generally be warm in the day and cool at night – although older buildings that lack adequate insulation will release some of their warmth back into the atmosphere – and they'll be very hot in summer and very cold in winter.

wind

Extreme temperatures and lack of shade are often compounded by one of the most damaging and annoying aspects of the weather – wind. Buildings offer shelter, as do hedges and fences, but up on a roof, if there's a gale blowing, we and our plants will very soon know about it.

Trellis screens and shelter planting will go some way towards dissipating wind but plants that reach any appreciable size will be at the mercy of all the elements, all of their lives. For this reason we need to choose them with care, confining our selection to those that can cope with such situations and preferably those that relish them. A long season of interest is also important, along with some evergreen plants for winter display.

Develop the roof into an outdoor room and you'll soon wonder how you lived without it.

cultivation

All plants will need to be grown in containers as large as possible to allow extensive root growth and cut down on maintenance. Even small trees, multi-stemmed for extra impact, will thrive in large tubs if kept well fed and watered. Add a structure of shrubs as a permanent framework and enhanced with seasonal bedding, herbs and bulbs.

irrigation

A large collection of pots in a place where access may be limited could call for some form of automatic irrigation. In summer, the sunshine and warm winds will dry things out pretty quickly, probably making it essential. It's also an effective way of minimizing the amount of water that physically needs carting around.

A drip irrigation system is probably the best solution. Allowing accurate and controlled delivery of water to each plant, it can be linked to a timer and fully automated for ease and peace of mind. It may also be possible to collect natural rainfall from adjacent roofs in water butts. Of course, it isn't wise to interfere with existing drainage, but quite often there will be sections of roof without gutters that previously shed their water into the space now occupied by the garden.

Once you've sorted out the structural requirements, you can grow almost anything on a roof.

roofs for living

As an escape from the outside world or as an extension to the home, roofs offer valuable additional living space. The design of any garden space should take into account the role it is going to play, and roofs are no exception. For entertaining there will need to be an area for a table and chairs. Shade may also be required – provided by plants trained over a pergola, small trees or a garden umbrella. Lights will transform the garden at night and may serve a functional role for extra safety. Low-voltage systems are easy to install, but everything will require a power supply from indoors so consult a qualified electrician.

Storage is also useful for tools and equipment and the easiest option is to add a small shed or storage box. The more competent DIYer may decide something 'built-in' makes better use of space and is less obtrusive, disguised perhaps as some form of seating.

glowing globes

For a roof space that's to be enjoyed by night, how about making some globe lights? Using the same principle of back-to-back hanging baskets, it's possible to make some fun and effective light sculptures. They are the perfect complement to your growing globes.

you will need:

galvanized wire baskets

galvanized 'chicken' wire mesh

fine galvanized wire

fairy lights designed for use
  outside

pliers

tin snips

At dusk the glowing globes will really come alive. Place them on a reflective surface for a magical effect.

1 Cut off a length of chicken wire using the tin snips. Watch the cut ends as they're sharp. You may prefer to wear gloves.

2 Scrunch the chicken wire into a rough ball shape, taking care not to crush it too much.

3 Gradually build up the ball by adding more and more layers of wire mesh until it's roughly the same size as the hanging basket.

WARNING Only use low-voltage lights specifically designed for exterior use.

4 Starting with the end bulb, carefully wrap the fairly lights around the mesh ball, making sure they are evenly distributed across the whole surface.

5 Trap the mesh ball and lights in between the two galvanized baskets.

6 Wire the two baskets together with fine galvanized wire.

roof plant gallery

grasses

Ornamental grasses have certainly caught our imagination, probably because they're easy to grow and are attractive for most of the year. They also thrive in pots and containers.

Grouped together with sedges and rushes, many are evergreen, some annual and the rest perennial. Maintenance is minimal, with an occasional trim to remove dead leaves and faded flower stems. Watering is important in hot, dry weather although most true grasses hate being waterlogged.

Many of the evergreen varieties change their looks throughout the year, turning rich browns and bronzes in winter, looking all the better for a dusting of snow or powdery coat of frost. These are architectural plants that lend themselves to any situation.

ten for pots…

Acorus gramineus (Japanese rush)
This is not strictly a grass, but it is grass-like in appearance and thrives in moist soil conditions. Long thick leaves are semi-evergreen and a rich glossy green. For pale green and cream stripes choose the variety 'Ogon'.

Briza maxima (quaking grass) An annual grass which produces attractive straw-coloured seedheads that stand well and quake in the breeze.

Carex buchananii (leatherleaf sedge) Beautiful orange-brown evergreen leaves that twist at the tip.

Carex hachijoensis 'Evergold' Cream-and-green-edged evergreen leaves on a mound-forming plant.

Carex testacea Another evergreen grass with pale green arching leaves that turn a rich bronze in full sun.

Hakonechloa macra 'Aureola' A superb deciduous grass with green-striped, bright yellow leaves that become flushed pink in autumn. Best in partial shade.

Imperata cylindrica 'Rubra' A perennial grass with leaves that emerge green and quickly turn blood-red from their tips down to the base. It is a spreading plant and doesn't like the cold and wet together so may appreciate a dry winter mulch.

Stipa arundinacea (pheasant's tail grass) This is a lovely evergreen grass with feathery flowerheads in summer and early autumn.

Stipa tenuissima A deciduous grass with a very erect habit. Flowerheads are white, turning brown in autumn. This is an excellent grass for providing movement in a breeze.

Uncinia rubra A dwarf sedge with stiff, reddish-brown, curved leaves and black flowers in late summer.

TIP Sounds are important to stimulate all the senses. Rustling grasses will do this, so long as the breeze is reasonably gentle.

Above: *Carex hachijoensis* 'Evergold' will thrive in a warm, sunny and free-draining location, so is ideal for a rooftop location.

TIP Use the polystyrene chips employed as protection in packaging in the base of planters, instead of crocks. A reasonable layer will maintain good drainage but weigh less than damp compost so large planters are as light as possible and may still be moved around with ease.

conifers

Somewhat out of fashion, conifers are perfect for all-year-round colour and interest – especially if space is at a premium. As a specimen plant in a large container, they'll add drama and impact to any porch, courtyard, balcony or roof terrace.

worth looking out for...

Abies concolor 'Compacta' (dwarf white fir) Beautiful steel-blue branches are carried on a compact tree.

Cedrus libani 'Sargentii' (dwarf cedar) This has elegant weeping branches covered in blue-green needles. Slow growing and easy to train.

Chamaecyparis pisifera 'Filifera Aurea' (sawara cypress) This cypress has whip-like golden foliage. The blue-green variety 'Boulevard' does well in a pot, provided it is kept moist.

Juniperus x *pfitzeriana* (juniper) A good dwarf juniper with a wealth of interesting varieties to choose from. Look out for golden 'Pfitzeriana Aurea', mottled 'Blue and Gold', and 'Gold Coast', which is even more compact.

Juniperus sabina var. *tamariscifolia* (juniper) A lovely spreading juniper. Plant it to cascade down the side of a large pot.

Pinus mugo (dwarf mountain pine) Pines cope well with heat and light and this is a dwarf form for a large pot. Look out for 'Gnom', which forms a spreading tree, and 'Mops', a real miniature. For added colour try 'Ophir' – its needles turn yellow in winter.

Sciadopitys verticillata (umbrella pine) An unusual and ultimately large conifer but very slow growing. The needles take on bright yellow autumn and winter tints.

Taxus baccata 'Repens Aurea' (golden spreading yew) A yew that has yellow-edged needles on branches that sprawl over raised beds and from tall planters.

Left: Even in winter *Pinus mugo* 'Ophir' provides a splash of colour.

fruit

Tree and soft fruit are more difficult than vegetables to grow in a confined space – but not impossible. Pears, peaches, nuts and raspberries are all too vigorous, but it's worth having a try with apples, strawberries or grapes. This is a good way to grow something attractive, and then enjoy it on a plate.

consider...

Apples Grown on a dwarfing rootstock, a small apple tree will make an attractive potted focal point. Trained as cordons or espaliers, they can also dress up a boring wall.

Blackberries Vigorous and thorny although thornless varieties are available. Trained along a fence or over a door, they could provide a decent crop, but should be combined with something more decorative for floral appeal.

Blueberries Delicious and decorative, blueberries will thrive in a large pot of ericacous compost. They also put on a good show of autumn colour.

Currants The plants of both red and white look superb when they're dripping with berries. Standard-trained plants are expensive but look brilliant.

Figs A large-leaved tree with delicious fruits that can take a year to ripen so may need protection during the winter. They'll ripen quicker against a sunny wall.

Gooseberries Bright green or plum-purple fruits on spiny plants. Again cordon and standard plants make delicious focal points.

Grapes With decorative leaves that can provide welcome shade, a grape vine is well worth considering. Crops can be variable and of dubious culinary use although they're perfect for home-made wine.

Strawberries These are perhaps the most decorative and delicious fruit of all. A few plants can be used to edge a large pot and the fruit will hang down the sides until it's ripe – assuming we can get to it before the birds.

Left: Delicious sun-ripened figs, a treat for any gardener.

vegetables

There are a large number of vegetables that will thrive in containers. Most vegetables need plenty of sun so choose a bright spot. Pests and diseases should be minimal as you're so far away from other gardens.

likely candidates...

Aubergines A tropical plant and therefore one for a very sheltered warm spot. The deep purple fruit are attractive and should only be picked when they turn shiny.

Courgettes Excellent large leaves, and the more courgettes you cut, the more will grow.

Dwarf or French beans These have the taste of runners, without using the space. The foliage is pretty and the pods quite decorative – particularly if you choose a purple-podded variety.

Lettuce This salad crop is easily sown in situ or raised as young plants on a windowsill and planted out among ornamentals. Try the leaf varieties rather than the hearting types – they're more decorative and easier to grow.

Peppers In shades of red, yellow, green and purple, sweet peppers are ornamental and delicious. The plants are small and easy to squeeze in among other plants.

Pumpkins and squashes With their trailing vines, these can be most decorative and are perfect for softening the edges of containers. Fruits may need supporting, if they get heavy, and they should be picked before they get too large.

Radish A quick to grow and a tasty addition to soups and salads. The roots are ready for pulling just a few weeks after sowing.

Ruby chard For decorative leaves and stems, ruby chard is hard to beat – a particularly decorative addition to pots and tubs.

Shallots Smaller than onions and easier to grow, shallot bulbs multiply during the summer and can be harvested in autumn.

Sweet corn Corn produces large feature plants that take very little space. They're wind-pollinated, so you need a group to have any edible cobs.

Tomatoes Well worth growing for their large red or yellow ornamental fruits. Dwarf plants will do well in pots or trailing out of hanging baskets. The small 'cherry' varieties will produce a good crop in a limited space.

Sweet peppers are easy to grow and produce delicious fruit.

sun-lovers

Many plants thrive in seemingly hostile conditions. On a roof, where there is often plenty of sunshine, but where things can get a little hot and dry in the summer, plants need to look after themselves.

a dozen that relish just such conditions...

Allium christophii (ornamental onion) This onion has large purple globes of flowers that also dry well.

Anthemis tinctoria (golden marguerite) Ferny foliage above which is borne a mass of daisy flowers in summer and autumn. Look out for 'E.C. Buxton' a lemon-yellow variety.

Cistus x *cyprius* (rock rose) A shrubby perennial with evergreen leaves and pure white flowers with yellow and red centres.

Euonymus fortunei 'Emerald 'n' Gold' A shrub with golden-yellow evergreen leaves, spreading habit and bronze winter tints.

Euphorbia characias subsp. *wulfenii* A magnificent evergreen with large lime-green mopheads of flowers in spring lasting well throughout the summer.

Euryops pectinatus This plant has evergreen, silvery, fern-like foliage with bright yellow daisy flowers from midsummer into autumn.

Oenothera biennis (evening primrose) This free-flowering biennial has large golden cup-shaped flowers that open in the evening and seem to float as the foliage can't be seen in the dark. 'Lemon Sunset' has softer yellow flowers, fading to pink-red.

Olearia phlogopappa (daisy bush) An evergreen shrub with wavy-edged leaves, smothered in white daisy flowers in spring.

Origanum laevigatum (marjoram) Fragrant leaves and attractive pink flowers from late spring through to autumn.

Phlomis fruticosa (Jerusalem sage) An evergreen shrub with aromatic silver leaves and yellow flower spikes in summer.

Phlox subulata (moss phlox) A free flowering evergreen producing carpets of pink, white or mauve in spring, depending on the variety.

Stachys lanata (lamb's ears) A low-grower with woolly silver evergreen leaves and summer flower spikes. Excellent for using as ground-cover and for softening pot edges.

Above left: Thriving in a warm dry spot, the ornamental onion *Allium christophii* has flowers that last for several months.
Right: Bursting with flavour and happy in a pot, ruby chard is a must.

black

This is one of the most interesting colours to use in a planting scheme, as a focal point, contrast or conversation piece.

some excellent black plants...

Ajuga reptans 'Braunherz' (purple-leaved bugle) Rich dark purple evergreen foliage that spreads to give year-round interest. Deep blue flowers from mid-spring to early summer. Ideal for containers as ground-cover or an edging.

Alcea rosea 'Nigra' A superb black-flowered hollyhock for sheltered corners or against a sheltered wall. The large, single flowers have a pale yellow throat.

Alocasia sanderiana A tender exotic with large arrow-shaped leaves that are black with contrasting silver veins. Needs winter protection.

Colocasia esculenta 'Black Magic' An exotic plant that likes moist conditions but will need moving indoors for the winter. The leaves are large and almost pure black.

Cornus alba 'Kesselringii' (black dogwood) A large shrub with black winter stems. Also good for autumn colour when its leaves turn red and purple.

Euphorbia amygdaloides 'Purpurea' (purple-leaved spurge) The evergreen leaves are deep purple, and bright yellow flowers appear in summer. Happy in sun or shade.

Ophiopogon planiscapus 'Nigrescens' Often referred to as 'the black grass', this is not a grass at all but a member of the lily family. The leaves are thin and almost black. Mauve flowers in summer are followed by blue-black berries.

Tradescantia pallida 'Purple Heart' An excellent evergreen ground cover with deepest purple-black foliage that produces the best colour in full sun. Small pink flowers in summer.

Ophiopogon planiscapus 'Nigrescens' is great for a colour contrast but needs thoughtful planting to avoid being lost among brighter companions.

care

Making a beautiful garden in various places around the home is only half the story. That's the creative bit where we can enhance our living environment and exhibit our personal taste and style. Now we come to the real gardening bit, caring for what we've created to make sure it stays in good condition and achieves its full potential.

Almost all the projects we've looked at involve containers. This means that most of the plants we are growing will be totally dependent on us for their survival. However, assuming plants have an in-built desire to survive, which they do, and a tolerance of slight errors of judgement by the novice gardener, which they also do, we only need to carry out a few basic tasks to keep everything happy and healthy.

With most hobbies, it's possible to go into the subject to varying degrees of depth. Gardening is no exception and as experience levels increase, and confidence is gained, novice gardeners will very soon become experts at looking after the plants in their charge. As the months go by there will be a natural tendency to try new plants and techniques and this is how the gardening bug usually germinates. Seeing what others achieve in their own homes, visiting large flower shows and keeping an eye on what's happening in garden centres will inevitably lead to a desire to try something new for ourselves. However, the initial problem is to keep the plants we have fit and well, and to do this we need to master a range of simple skills. Rather like housework, there are some jobs that really must be done on a regular basis, and others that are good if we have the time and inclination, but are not absolutely necessary.

essential jobs

Although the galleries highlight plants that can cope with the often extreme conditions faced by the 'no-garden gardener', the plants themselves still need planting in the right way if they're to survive.

planting

First and foremost is the container, which should be clean and as large as possible. Into this add a drainage layer of broken crocks or gravel. Plant roots need air as well as water and the crocks make sure the compost doesn't become waterlogged. Polystyrene packing chips are also effective and particularly good for roofs and balconies and other sites where we're aiming to keep weight to a minimum. Tender and evergreen plants can be give extra winter protection by lining containers with insulation material prior to planting. Foam filler works well, but can be a little messy. Plastic bubble packaging film is also good and long lasting.

how it's done

Always use good quality potting compost and add extra grit, perlite or vermiculite to improve drainage but retain moisture. Large shrubs and trees will be happier in a loam-based compost and its extra weight provides stability in windy conditions. Smaller plants, bedding, bulbs and annuals will be fine in a loamless compost, which is lighter (again ideal for roofs and balconies) and more pleasant to handle.

Fill the container with compost, firming it lightly. Compost compresses with time, so it's

> **PLANTING TIPS**
> - Check over new plants to see that they're free of all pests and diseases and remove any small weeds that may also occupy their pot.
> - Fill containers with as many plants as possible for a more instant effect. It's fine to over-plant as they'll be being fed and watered regularly.
> - Plant at the same level as they were in their nursery pot.
> - Use a decorative mulch to cover the surface of the compost – this keeps in moisture and stops compost splashing the plants.

important to firm it periodically as the pot is being filled. Fail to do this and the plants will gradually sink below the rim of the pot over the coming weeks. It's also worth mentioning that the final compost level should be a little way under the rim as this will make watering much easier.

Next it's time to place the plants, largest first and then filling in around these. Plants that have been on the nursery for some time, or are particularly vigorous, will have completely filled their pots with roots. Left like this, they may never branch into the new compost so gently tease a few out to give them a helping hand.

All plants should be well watered before planting. Surprisingly, a dry rootball can stay bone dry, even when it's planted into moist compost. Plunging pots into the kitchen sink or a bucket of water is the best way of making sure everything's as it should be.

Plants should end up at the same depth they were in their pots. Planted too deep or too shallow and they'll either die or struggle to become established. Firm again using your fingertips as these apply the right amount of pressure, and then water well to settle the soil around the roots.

hardening off

Many of the plants we buy from garden centres, particularly bedding plants designed to provide a temporary splash of colour, will have been raised in polythene tunnels or greenhouses. This ensures they grow rapidly and are in perfect condition when they reach the stores. However, they then need time to adjust to changes in temperature and light so a intermediate process called 'hardening off' is needed once we get them home. This is particularly true of the tender plants that nurseries and garden centres sell in early spring, several months before it's safe for them to go outside. Planted straight out into outdoor containers, they'll be dead in a matter of hours.

It's best to acclimatize any spring purchase to it's new environment by standing it out where it's going to go during the day, and then bringing it back into a cool room at night. Do this for a couple of weeks, by which time it

will have hardened off and will be ready for final planting. Plants bought during the rest of the year are not so problematic although any new purchase should be treated with care.

aftercare

Many container plants outgrow their pots over a number of years. Tell-tale signs are roots coming out of the drainage holes, reduced vigour and a plant that always seems to need watering. Potting on into larger pots, following the same planting procedure is essential to maintain a plant's well-being.

root pruning

If there comes a point where containers are as big as they can be, do a little light root pruning. Knock the plant out of its pot and gently brush away some of the soil to expose the outer fibrous roots, which you can then cut back with sharp secateurs. Once the rootball has been reduced in size, the plant can be popped back into its pot and back-filled with fresh compost.

top dressing

Another good idea is to top-dress pots each spring. This involves scraping away the surface layer and replacing it with fresh compost. Plants treated in this way will receive a welcome boost of fresh nutrients and the pots will look tidy and cared for.

It's important to let plants acclimatize to their new environment before planting them out.

Water well, and water less frequently.

watering

The area of watering, or watering properly, is where most gardeners can get it wrong. Whether from absent-mindedness or a lack of understanding of specific requirements, most plants die because they're over- or under watered. It's a mistake that the novice gardener is bound to make.

A good rule of thumb is: 'water well and water less frequently'. A thorough drenching will make sure that all the compost in a container gets wet. Plant roots will be encouraged to spread out into the whole container and then make full use of the compost and nutrients available. Plants will then be more drought-resistant, having extensive and effective root systems. Such well-watered containers can then be left for longer between waterings as the compost should be left to dry out to prevent roots from rotting. Roots need air as well as moisture.

Those who adopt a 'little and often' regime are making a rod for their own backs. Applying a little water will only wet the surface layer of compost and encourages the plant's roots to stay shallow. Here they're more prone to drought and less likely to make full use of the nutrients available. They'll also need rewatering far more frequently.

Of course, where the containers are positioned will dramatically affect the frequency with which they need watering, so will their size and the number and type of plants they contain. Those in warm, sunny locations that may also be breezy will require more attention than those in a sheltered, shady spot.

feeding

All plants need nutrients and most of these will be available from the compost they're growing in, at least initially. Many modern potting composts contain slow-release fertilizers that will be available to the plants for the first six months of growth. However, very vigorous growth can use these up quickly, as does the fact that we've put a large number of plants into a relatively small volume of compost. The answer is to supply supplementary feeds in the form of fertilizer.

A good place to start is with a 'balanced general-purpose' fertilizer.

These contain a blend of all the nutrients the plants may need. Such feeds can be applied in solid or liquid form, the latter is easy to do when we're watering anyway and has a more immediate effect.

Feed once a fortnight or every month as a matter of course. The trick is to establish a routine, starting in spring as plant growth resumes and finishing in early autumn as they shed their leaves or stop growing for the winter. This way the plants will maintain their vigour throughout the whole season.

As you gain experience and a desire to encourage specific plants to perform, look at fertilizers designed to achieve specific results. If you're after flowers then look for something high in potash as this will encourage flower bud production. If, however, it's lush foliage you want, then a high-nitrogen fertilizer will have the desired effect.

pruning

A bit of a nightmare for those growing masses of fruit trees or beds of roses, but for the 'no garden gardener', pruning is a case of using common sense. First, if something gets so vigorous it's obscuring a door or hanging over a window, then simply cut it off. Regardless of the season or type of plant, it simply has to go. This is also true for variegated plants when they produce a plain green shoot. This should be cut out, well back down into the main body of the plant. Plain green shoots are always more vigorous and would grow rapidly at the expense of the rest of the plant.

Second, don't be afraid to prune. Remember that the harder we prune, the more vigorous the new growth will be. So, quite the opposite to what you might expect, a plant that seems a little lethargic and reluctant to grow should be pruned hard. Conversely, a vigorous shrub or climber should be only lightly

pruned to keep it within bounds. Obviously there are exceptions and common sense should prevail, but it's something we should have in the back of our minds.

pests & diseases

There comes a time when every new gardener realizes they're sharing their plants with some uninvited guests. Insect pests and fungal diseases will inevitably put in an appearance and if left untreated could quickly decimate the entire display. Healthy plants are far less prone to problems, so the best stance to take is one of prevention so any problems are quickly identified and dealt with before they reach epidemic proportions. Make regular visual checks, paying particular attention to soft new shoots and the undersides of leaves

pests...

Unlike in a conventional garden, the few plants in our care all have a vital role to play. In a large border, an aphid-laden marigold can be forgiven as it will be lost among the others: this is not the case in our 'garden', where the marigold might be one of very few plants. We also don't have the option of planting much in the way of wildlife-attracting plants that will encourage natural predators. However, as we're working on a small scale, physical control is much simpler. Picking off slugs, snails, aphids and scale insects isn't the most pleasant occupation, but nip them in the bud and they'll not have a chance of doing much damage or multiplying either.

slugs and snails will eat new, succulent shoots and fleshy leaves. Pick them off by hand or use a proprietary slug killer. Slugs and snails can also be discouraged by physical barriers such as sharp sand or grit, or a layer of petroleum jelly around the rim of the container.

vine weevil is a major container pest. The white grubs live in the soil and eat the plant's roots; the adults eat the leaves. Chemical controls are available. These are watered onto the soil, killing the weevils and grubs as they feed. You can also buy special container composts that contain an effective chemical control.

aphids and blackfly, despite their minute scale, can cause major problems sucking the sap from, and distorting, new shoots and leaves. A systemic insecticide that actually travels within the plant will control them, as will organic soft soap sprays or those based on natural pyrethrums.

scale insects live on woody stems and again require chemical control, or picking off by hand.

greenfly also attack new shoots but can be controlled with insecticides, organic sprays based on natural pyrethrums or soft soap.

earwigs will eat holes in flower petals. Chemical controls are available or the insects can be trapped in upturned flowerpots stuffed with newspaper.

diseases...

Diseases are less of a problem than insect pests, but their effects can be alarmingly dramatic. A mould can wipe out a whole tray of

seedlings overnight or cause a plant to collapse in a couple of days. Good hygiene is important as both pests and diseases live in dead leaves and on old decaying stems. Problems are also more likely to occur if plants are overfed, overwatered or overcrowded.

There are fungicide sprays that will deal with most problems but as diseases are often swift-acting, it can already be too late before you even identify the problem. The obvious answer is to get the watering, feeding and planting conditions just right and a lot of diseases will never arise. As it rarely recovers, remove any plant material that's showing signs of illness and put it in the bin.

botrytis is a grey mould that attacks seedlings, stems, leaves and flowers in damp conditions. Remove infected materials and increase air flow.

damping off, when seedlings collapse, indicates they were sown too thickly and the soil is too wet.

mildew appears as a white or yellow powdery mould and is caused by dry roots. Watering and mulching to conserve moisture will help.

PRUNING

- Always cut to just above a bud so a new shoot will form where the old one was.
- Never leave a section of stem without any buds as it will die back and allow disease into the rest of the plant.
- Make cuts that slope away from the bud so rainwater is shed to one side.
- Use a sharp pair of secateurs that will leave neat cuts which are less likely to become diseased.

PESTS AND DISEASES

- Buy ready-to-use sprays as these are easier to handle and store.
- Always follow the manufacturer's recommendations and keep all chemicals away from children and animals.

if there's time...

The great thing about gardening is that it's a hobby with which we can achieve spectacular results with very little knowledge. Of course, as our interest deepens we'll discover a bottomless pit of facts, techniques and skills. So the keen potential gardener who wants to spend more time caring for their plants may like to consider the following...

cleaning

Inner city areas, and most major towns and cities, have a problem with atmospheric pollution. It's a fact of life and something our plants have to put up with, too. Plants by a front door and on a balcony or roof are particularly susceptible to all the dust and grime that comes their way, blown by the wind or brought down with the rain.

Without getting too technical and wrapped up in a botanical explanation, it's important to know that plants live and breathe through their leaves and stems. They use light to grow and make essential nutrients and if anything stops this light getting to the leaves then their health will soon begin to suffer. Similarly, their leaves are used for gaseous exchange, whereby they use atmospheric carbon dioxide and release oxygen back into the environment. Again, if anything coats the leaf surface or undersides and clogs up the special pores that do this, the plant will also start to die.

We spend much of our time cleaning around our homes, and this activity is no longer confined to spring. However bad it seems, a layer of dust on top of a cupboard is hardly a life-threatening situation, but for our plants dust can, indeed, be fatal. And in and around the home, large specimen plants need to be maintained in tip-top condition if they are to fulfil their role as a focal point or centrepiece in a room. Covered in dust they'll certainly get noticed, but for all the wrong reasons.

In short, plants need cleaning. Of course those outside get washed by natural rainfall which removes much of the dirt, but in and around our homes pollutants are much more prevalent and our plants will need a helping hand. It's a good idea to give them a shower. If they're small and portable this can be done in the bathroom, so long as the water's tepid not hot. This washes most of the dust off the leaves (and means the bathroom needs cleaning again). It will also restore something of the plant's natural colour and shine.

Houseplants can also be cleaned with proprietary leaf shine sprays and wipes available from garden centres and DIY stores. These remove the dirt leaving behind an oily film that makes leaves look lush and glossy. Be very careful though as this oily film can also clog the leaf pores, so shines and wipes should only be used on naturally tough or glossy leaves. Anything delicate or particularly fine should be given a shower instead.

Hairy-leaved plants, cacti and succulents are more problematic, the hairs often trapping more dust than their smoother counterparts. Here a soft paint brush works wonders, enabling you to flick away the dust, cobwebs and dead flies. Some people even use a vacuum cleaner with a piece of fabric over the nozzle. Again, it's effective at removing dust but requires some confidence and a steady hand.

And what about the pots themselves? These should also be kept clean to discourage pests and diseases and make sure they look attractive. And if they're not going to be used until next year, don't leave them outside over the winter still full of old compost. Do this and the compost will get saturated and when it then freezes it will expand and could crack the pot.

If storage space is a problem, the pots can be left outside, but should be emptied and given a thorough wash and scrub with detergent.

deadheading

Flowering plants are great until the flowers start to fade: very soon that spectacular red azalea will be covered in withered brown remains and others can be just as bad. Although it can be time-consuming, removing dead flowers is a good way of tidying up the plants and preventing them from wasting energy by producing seed. Some seedheads are attractive so the faded flowers should be left in the interests of a further display. But on the whole, if a flower dies, it's best removed so the plants can concentrate on making new shoots and developing more flower buds for next year.

training

Pruning is a necessary evil, but it can also be done for purely aesthetic reasons – when it is called training – rather than out of necessity. Topiary evergreens will need regular trimming if their shapes are to be maintained or developed. Hand shears and secateurs do the job well, maintaining the degree of control that's necessary for pinpoint accuracy. Most evergreens can be trimmed two or three times during the summer while growth is most vigorous. This also means they have the autumn to recover and toughen up their new shoots ready for winter.

propagation

Finally, to one of the most interesting, and potentially addictive gardening activities of all: propagation. Nature is an amazing thing and when it comes to reproducing plants, all we need to do is provide a helping hand. The ability of a shoot to produce new roots will always amaze even the most knowledgeable gardener. For the novice, it's nothing short of a miracle.

from seeds…

The cheapest way of producing a large number of plants is to grow them from seed. Mail order specialists, garden centres and supermarkets offer an ever-increasing array, and many are not difficult to grow. All will have been specially raised, graded, sorted and packaged so they're as fresh as possible and will grow true to type.

That term 'true to type' is worth looking at in more detail. Not all seeds will produce plants exactly the same as the parent. Many gardeners collect seed from their own plants, sow it and then are surprised when the resulting plants bear little similarity to the original. This is because seeds are the result of sexual reproduction and with the birds and bees involved there's no knowing where the pollen has come from. It may be from the plant next door, or one many miles away. Commercial seed manufacturers grow their seed plants in such large quantities and controlled conditions that this isn't really a problem.

We also now have plants referred to as F_1 hybrids and these are noted for their improved vigour and

uniformity. They are the results of controlled pollination, so the exact parentage is known. Of course, all the science means that the seeds are more expensive, but it's a price worth paying in the interests of ease and guaranteed success.

There is now a good selection of windowsill propagators on the market, so it's no longer necessary to have a greenhouse if you want to raise your own plants. Even a pot standing on a windowsill or balcony with a piece of glass over the top creates the perfect conditions for germination. Many, such as the hardy and half-hardy annuals, can also be sown directly where they are to grow. Simply scattering them on the surface of the compost and keeping them well watered is all that's necessary.

All seeds need minimum

Above: Growing from seed is fascinating and requires little in the way of space, expertise or expenditure.

Left: Foliage plants such as hostas really benefit from a wash now and then.

temperatures before they germinate. For most plants, the warmth of a windowsill is usually sufficient. Those that like it really warm will need a spell in a heated propagator to get them started. Some seeds also need special treatment to encourage them to germinate more quickly. This may be a spell in the refrigerator, a slight cut in the seed coat or soaking overnight in warm water. Seed packets are a mine of useful information and will usually indicate when some form of special treatment is needed. Some seeds are even sold pre-germinated.

GENERAL PROPAGATION TIPS

■ Keep everything spotlessly clean, so rots and moulds don't kill young plants when they're at their most vulnerable.

■ Follow the instructions on seed packets – they're written by experts who want us to get the best possible results.

■ Use fresh compost for all propagation, so it's not contaminated in any way.

■ Be patient. Many a seedling or cutting has failed because it's been pricked out too early or tugged one time too many to see if it's rooted.

■ Never take cuttings or seed from other people's plants without permission. Garden visiting is not a licence to fill pockets and bags with free plants.

establish in their new pots and make sure they're hardened off before they're planted outside.

Left: Bamboos can be divided using a small saw to cut through the roots.
Right: A little care and attention will ensure that plants such as these miniature irises, called 'Harmony', perform to their full potential.

There's a tendency to sow too thickly and then seedlings suffer as they fight for space and nutrients, becoming leggy and more difficult to handle. Sow thinly and evenly, and the problem will not arise. Remember to label everything as it's sown, as one pot of seedlings looks very much like another.

When it's time to pot up, usually when the first set of true leaves have been produced, always handle the seedlings by their leaves, never by the stem or roots: a young plant can easily produce a new leaf, but has trouble doing anything about a crushed stem or damaged. Keep a close eye on your plants as they

from cuttings…

There's a lot of myth and mystery associated with gardening, which can, and often does, completely baffle the novice. Gardening is not an exact science. There are so many variables involved that what works for one person may not work for the next. The technique of propagating by cuttings is a good example: there are 101 ways of doing exactly the same thing. All have their merits and after you've spent a few seasons experimenting, you'll find a way the suits your skills and needs.

Basically, taking a cutting is a way of producing a new plant that will be identical in every way to the parent. For this reason, it's essential only to propagate from strong shoots that exhibit the typical characteristics of the type – the correct amount of variegation, for example, or the shape of the individual leaves. From these healthy shoots, it's possible to encourage new roots to grow. There are several types of cutting taken at different times of year, but the two most common are softwood and semi-ripe. The terms relate to the condition of the shoot when the cutting is taken and each will need handling in a slightly different way.

Different plants respond to propagation in different ways and for some softwood cuttings will work best while others do better from semi-ripe. Again what works well for one person will not work for another so a little trial and error is needed. But with something that takes very little time, and occupies such a small amount of space, it's well worth trying.

- **Softwood cuttings** are taken in the spring when the plant's new shoots are fully developed and just starting to harden. Although they're more prone to wilting, young shoots are most willing to produce roots, so many of the more difficult plants are propagated in this way. The tendency to wilt means they need to be kept in a humid atmosphere but a simple windowsill propagator or just a polythene bag over the pot is usually sufficient, so long as the cuttings are kept out of direct sunlight.
- **Semi-ripe cuttings** are taken in late summer and are less prone to wilting than softwood ones as the stem tissues will have hardened and become woody. Shoots should have grown in the current year and it is best to choose side shoots as they'll be firm at the base but still soft at the tip.
- **For both softwood and semi-ripe cuttings** remove the cutting from the main stem, cutting cleanly and as close to it as possible. Make each cutting 10–15cm (4–6in) long and remove the bottom leaves.

Cut a sliver of bark from the base of the cutting, to make it more likely to produce new roots. Dip in hormone rooting powder or gel and insert in a pot of special cuttings compost. Firm, water and label. Place softwood cuttings in a propagator or mist unit or cover with a plastic bag; place semi-ripe cuttings outside in a cool, sheltered spot – perhaps at the base of a shady wall. The cuttings should have rooted by spring, when they can be potted up or planted out.

by division…

One of the easiest and most satisfying ways of producing plants is by dividing what we already have. Perennials are a prime example: frequently the plant can be lifted, cut into several portions and then replanted. This is a good way of keeping plants healthy as they can become congested with old shoots and roots and the soil they're in can become tired and starved of nutrients. Lifting and dividing means that both these problems can be addressed. Only the young vigorous portions should be replanted and the soil can be improved with compost and fertilizer before you replant. Division is best done just as the plants start to re-grow after their period of winter dormancy.

plants for free…

Some plants produce baby plants without the slightest bit of human intervention. Some will be

---

CUTTINGS TIPS

- Take cuttings early in the day when shoots are firm.
- All cuttings should be prepared with a clean, sharp knife.
- Prepare the cuttings and get them into the compost as quickly as possible after they've been collected, otherwise they'll start to wilt and die.
- Label everything, along with the date they were taken, so there's less of a temptation to tug at them to see if they've rooted.

produced on runners that root back into the ground, as in the case of strawberries and spider plants. Others produce miniature baby plants on the back of mature leaves, as is the case with the piggyback plant (*Tolmiea menzesii*). These plantlets can be potted up and grown on to replace their parents as they get too large or straggly, or given away to friends and relatives.

added protection

Although towns and cities are generally milder than the countryside, some of our more tender plants may need winter protection. Most traditional garden plants are what we call 'hardy'. That is, they'll survive temperatures down to as low as −15°C (5°F), much colder than we would find comfortable. 'Frost hardy' plants are happy down to about −5°C (23°F) while 'half hardy' ones will cope with 0°C (32°F). 'Frost tender' plants, which includes many of the now fashionable exotics, will only survive if winter temperatures are a minimum 5°C (41°F). This means they will need some form of winter protection if their survival is to be guaranteed.

People with garages, sheds or conservatories may consider bringing tender and less hardy plants indoors for the winter. It's a way of ensuring their survival, but can take up valuable space in a small, urban home. Protecting the plants in situ is the best alternative. The idea is to provide an insulating layer around the plant and keep it warm and dry. With perennials this could be in the form of a dry mulch of leaves or straw, spread over the top of the

container and anchored with some wire netting. Sand also works well. Larger, evergreen plants are more problematic – it's difficult to protect these and not create something of an eyesore. Cordylines, yuccas, tree ferns and palms will need to be surrounded with straw or bracken and an overcoat of horticultural fleece or hessian. The straw should be packed in around the shoots and leaves so the growing tips are well insulated, and this insulation should be checked several times during the winter. If the material gets wet, it can cause rotting so should be replaced. Only when the last frosts are over should the protection be removed.

composting

With several floors to negotiate, and refuse collections that seem to discriminate against garden rubbish, getting rid of prunings, weeds, leaves and dead flowers can be something of a problem in the centre of large towns and cities.

All good gardeners know that composting is the way forward. Not only is it environmentally sound, relieving pressure on landfill sites, it's also a way of returning to the soil the goodness that the plants remove as they grow. Well-rotted garden compost is hard to beat as a soil conditioner, and the deciding factor is often the realization that it's absolutely free.

Even a small rooftop garden can accommodate a compost heap, perhaps disguised in an attractive container. Thankfully, manufacturers are now aware that people with small gardens don't want to look at a few rough planks or an old plastic barrel. Now

they're producing bins that are smart and attractive, even disguised as something else. Beehives seem to be popular and are fine in an informal, cottagey setting, but for a more urban, contemporary look the bin is better disguised with sheet of steel or coloured Perspex.

COMPOSTING TIPS

- Place the bin somewhere where it will be out of the way, on a surface where it can drain freely but where access is easy.
- Cut everything up as small as possible so it rots down quickly.
- The compost bin needs to be moist for decomposition to take place, so water it if it gets dry in summer.
- A good compost heap will generate quite a bit of heat, which helps break down the rubbish and kills any weed seeds.
- Don't overload the bin with too much of one type of refuse. If you have a lot of prunings, mix them up with compost that's already started to rot.
- Add vegetable waste from the kitchen – it's another valuable source of organic matter.
- Use a compost accelerator to speed up the rotting process.
- Bins that get too hot will stop working, so shade them in summer under adjacent plantings or with a piece of old carpet.
- Bins that are too cold also stop working, so line the sides with insulation material during the winter if speed is of the essence.
- Leave the bin for at least six months, a year if possible, until the compost is dark and crumbly.

photographic acknowledgements

The publishers would like to thank the following for supplying photographs:

Clive Nichols Garden Pictures: pp2–3(Designer: Christopher Bradley-Hole), 4(Claire Mee/Candy Brothers Devt), 8–9, 10(Designer: Nina Thalinson), 11(The Nichols Garden, Reading), 12–13(Spidergarden.com, Chelsea 2000), 15(Designer: Ann Frith), 17(Wynniatt-Husey Clarke), 22–3(Designers: R. & J. Passmore), 24(Peter Reid), 26, 27(Greenhurst Garden, Sussex), 31rt(3rd&btm images)(The Nichols Garden, Reading), 32, 33left&btm rt, 34–5, 36–7(Andrew & Karla Jewell), 38left(Lucy Smith), 38–9(Sue Berger), 40(Brinsby College), 41top(Godstone Gardeners Club), 41btm(Stephen Woodhams), 46–7(Stiffkey, Chelsea 1994), 46(inset), 48–9, 50–1(main image)(Designers: R. &J. Passmore), 51rt(Andrew & Karla Jewell), 52(Designer: Vic Shanley), 53(Designer: Geoff Whiten, Chelsea 2000), 56, 57, 58–9, 60–1(Keeyla Meadows), 62–3(Andrew & Karla Jewell), 64(Dennis Fairweather), 65, 66(Wynniatt-Husey Clarke), 70left, 71rt, 72, 73, 74–5, 76–7(Clare Matthews), 79btm left(The Nichols Garden, Reading), 79ctre(Fiona Barratt), 79btm rt(John Simpson), 80, 81(Copton Ash, Kent), 85, 86–7, 90(Designer: Stephen Woodhams, Chelsea 2000), 94left, 102(Designer: Christian Wright), 103(Jonathan Baillie), 107(Fiona Barratt, 110, 111, 112–13, 114–15(Trevyn McDowell), 117, 118(Designer: Christopher Bradley-Hole for *Gardens Ilustrated*, Chelsea 1994), 119(Trevyn McDowell), 124, 125, 126, 127, 128–9, 133, 134, 136, 138(Wynniatt-Husey Clarke), 139

Flowerphotos: pp96–7(Dave Zubraski)

Garden Exposures Photo Library: pp104–5(Andrea Jones Location Photography/Channel 4 *Garden Doctors)*, 106(Channel 4 *Garden Doctors)*

Garden Picture Library: pp18–19(Phot: Brigitte Thomas), 27(Phot: Brigitte Thomas), 31rt(2nd image)(Phot: Lynne Brotchie), 33top rt(Phot: John Glover), 71left(Phot: Howard Rice), 90top(Phot: Friedrich Strauss), 91(Phot: Friedrich Strauss), 94rt(Phot: ZaraMcCalmont), 95left(Phot: Howard Rice), 95ctre(Phot: Clive Nichols), 95rt(Phot: A.I. Lord), 98–9(Phot: Friedrich Strauss, 101(Phot: Andrea Jones)

John Glover: pp31rt(topimage), 67

S. & O. Mathews: pp20–1, 70rt, 84, 100

Elizabeth Whiting Associates: pp88–9

Justyn Willsmore: pp6–7(main image), 28, 29, 30, 31left, 42–3, 44–5, 54, 55, 68, 69, 82, 83, 92, 93, 108, 109, 120, 121, 122, 123, 130–1, 137

index

Page numbers in **bold** type refer to main entries and projects; those in *italic* type refer to picture captions.